3-MINUTE HORSEMANSHIP

60 Amazingly Achievable Lessons to Improve Your Horse When Time Is Short

VANESSA BEE

Trafalgar Square
North Pomfret, Vermont

First published in 2014 by
Trafalgar Square Books
North Pomfret, Vermont 05053

Printed in China

Disclaimer of Liability
The author and publisher shall have neither liability nor responsibility to any person or entity with respect to any loss or damage caused or alleged to be caused directly or indirectly by the information contained in this book. While the book is as accurate as the author can make it, there may be errors, omissions, and inaccuracies.

Trafalgar Square Books encourages the use of approved safety helmets in all equestrian sports and activities.

Library of Congress Cataloging-in-Publication Data
Bee, Vanessa.
  3-minute horsemanship : 60 amazingly achievable lessons to improve your horse when time is short / Vanessa Bee.
     pages cm
  Includes index.
  ISBN 978-1-57076-620-6
  1. Horses--Training. 2. Horsemanship. I. Title. II. Title: Three-minute horsemanship.
  SF287.B368 2013
  636.1'0835--dc23
                              2013009920

All photographs by Philip Osborne except pp. 13 and 29 (bottom) by Bob Atkins and p. 147
    © Dusty Perin/www.dustyperin.com
Book design by Peter Holm, Sterling Hill Productions
Cover design by RM Didier
Typefaces: Calisto and Agenda

10 9 8 7 6 5 4 3 2 1

Dedication

This book is dedicated to all the horses
I have ever known—thank you for teaching me.

CONTENTS

PART TWO: IN THE SADDLE | 80

Ground Skills to Riding Skills—Making Life Simple! | 81

The 25 Ridden Exercises | 82

ACKNOWLEDGMENTS

My grateful thanks go to the team at Trafalgar Square Books for their continuing support and encouragement.

Thank you to Robert and Jacqueline McCormick of Kyogle, Australia, who started me on my horsemanship journey many years ago.

Thank you also to my husband, Philip, who took many of the photographs, and to my friends and their beautiful horses who helped by appearing in some of them. Thank you:

Clancy and Ziggy

Ray Squire, my farrier

Faye and Dan from the rescue organization P4P (people4ponies.co.uk)

Pauline and Topaz

Elaine and Chunky

Lord and Lady Leasefield and their horses Chunky and Buster

Julie and Rupert

Sue and Merry

Lesley and Bella

But most of all my greatest thanks go to Secret, the horse who has taught me so much—she is a horse in a million.

INTRODUCTION

HOW TO USE THIS BOOK

This book has been especially written for you, the time-starved, twenty-first-century horse owner. Day after day you make a promise to train yourself and your horse to be better at something, but when you get to the barn there just doesn't seem to be enough time.

Well, all this is about to change. Whether you are an accomplished horseman or a complete beginner, you will find that *3-Minute Horsemanship* is ideal when time is short.

Don't worry. I'm not going to tell you to read the book all the way through because I know you haven't got time! As you look through these pages you will see that there are three distinct Sections:

Part One: Ground Exercises. The first is devoted to demonstrating 35 *3-Minute Exercises*–all in hand to develop various skills.

Part Two: Ridden Exercises. The next 25 exercises are all performed on the horse's back.

Both Parts One and Two contain short, achievable tasks that can be built up—combined with others—to draw on when you are faced with a "real-life" more complicated challenge.

Part Three: Real Life Scenarios. Here are 20 commonly experienced challenges, which you can solve by using a combination of the exercises learned in Parts One and Two.

We often look at the big task and just give up because it seems too much to fit into our busy lives. In Part Three, I show you how to break any challenge down into small manageable exercises—without stress for you or your horse.

This is not a program; you are not ticking boxes before moving on.

Instead, you can dip into any one of the *3-Minute Exercises* and work on it that day because that's what you feel like doing. A few exercises need previous ones to help them get started, but mostly they work successfully when done on their own.

What really matters is the *quality* of the training and how you *finish* the session. Many of us give up because something isn't working. What message does that send to the horse? Not a good one, obviously. On the other hand, when we stop because an exercise *is* working, *we* feel good, *the horse* feels good, and there is another building block to success. It really is possible to carry out good-quality progressive training with your horse in only *three minutes a day* when you work in this way.

So when you have a specific training problem to solve, start by looking in Part Three at the *Real Life Scenarios*. But, if you just want to improve your horsemanship in a general way, you can dabble away to your heart's content in the Parts One and Two, and watch you and your horse really improve in just *three minutes a day*.

As you develop your ground work and riding techniques these movements will become more subtle until, to the onlooker, there seems to be no physical movement as you communicate with your horse. This book is not about classical equitation; it's a book about working with your horse in such a way that you both learn to work together quietly and harmoniously. Once this has been achieved you can start to work on the finer points of your horsemanship.

WHY "3" MINUTES?

It was while I was training my horses and ponies for Horse Agility that I began to notice that when the teaching session was short, ending on a positive note, the animals appeared to learn more quickly.

Due to my other work commitments, my daily training time was limited, so I would set small, achievable tasks for each horse to be sure that we could reach a positive conclusion in the time I had available. Because the question I asked of the horse was so simple, as soon as he had either completed the task, or made some headway toward achieving it, I would stop and reward him. I was amazed at how quickly the horses learned a new skill even though the sessions were so short. However, I became even more interested when I realized that when I set up a session with a realistic goal, *every* animal achieved that goal in less than three minutes.

I began to time my training sessions, being careful not to allow a three-minute time limit influence my instruction techniques or put either of us under pressure. I was also careful to vary the task from day to day, so that he did not become bored with the lessons. Again and again, I found that the animals were quietly working toward a successful conclusion and actually appeared to be learning more quickly.

In other words, my training time could sometimes be only a few seconds! I was always very careful not to get greedy and make each daily task more challenging: I just kept slowly building up to the bigger picture, patiently, with each exercise solid before I moved on.

Suddenly, training a horse at liberty to cross a tarpaulin in an open field became a reality. There was no discomfort, restraint or concern for either party. I was achieving *far more* than I ever believed possible by *doing far less* than I had ever done before.

I came to the conclusion that if I set a small achievable goal every day and worked toward it, stopping and rewarding when we were on the road to success—and not always when the goal was achieved—we moved on extremely quickly. If we didn't complete the exercise that day then it was because I had asked too much.

I taught my horse Secret, at liberty, to jump through a hoop in an open field in only a few minutes, but these minutes were spread over six days. I then researched this idea and found that in an experiment carried out in 1980 by a scientist called Rubin, ponies were trained in short sessions for either seven days, two days or one day a week. The results were surprising: The ponies that were trained for only one day a week achieved a higher level of performance—in fewer training sessions.

The study concluded that trainers should therefore keep a session short, work on a different skill each day, and stop drilling the horse after he has performed it.

By accident, I had discovered the secret! Short productive sessions over a longer period achieve better results. And so *3-Minute Horsemanship* was born.

HORSES SAY YES OR NO—*NEVER* MAYBE

What Makes a Horse a Horse?

It's a fact of life that a horse doesn't think like a human. He is often described as just an animal intent on eating grass for 18 hours a day, with short bursts of flight in order to avoid being eaten by a predator: a simple life for a free-living animal. But then, humans came along and complicated things!

In the wild a horse only needs to answer "Yes" or "No" to a simple question, such as "Should I run away?" However, we humans expect our horses to be more complex and considered in their reply: Instead of just saying "Yes" or "No," we imagine that the horse's thought process is more like: "Should I run or should I stand still? If I stand still, I risk being run down by a tractor, which must be dangerous because my rider feels afraid. I am afraid of the tractor, and my rider is afraid of the tractor, so why won't she let me run away?"

Can we expect horses to look at a complex situation, with many possible outcomes, and decide on one answer from many? I don't believe so. A flight animal such as a horse simply doesn't have time to think the situation through; he only has time to say "Yes" or "No."

Thousands, if not millions of years ago, horses that said "Maybe" didn't survive: They didn't reproduce and therefore died out. The only horses that survived were the ones that acted on their gut instinct and made a quick getaway before they became someone's lunch. The horse that held a long conversation about the health and safety aspects of running away simply didn't make it.

Think of a horse out for a ride when a plastic bag flies out of the hedge. He asks himself, "Should I run?" His evolutionary instincts tell him yes because he has been programmed that way: He will always run first and ask questions later.

It is the horse's life experiences that will influence his decision. A young or novice horse is more likely to answer "Yes" and make a run for it. The older horse may react instinctively initially and spook, but then quickly chooses not to run. In other words, he answers "No" because he has learned that bags are not dangerous.

How Do Horses Think?

To attribute a horse with the mental ability to do something deliberately annoying, and be stubborn or disrespectful, is giving him human characteristics that he cannot have. These characteristics require thought processes that involve planning ahead, something horses do not do. Horses do not store food for tomorrow or understand logical progression.

A simple experiment that illustrates this clearly was carried out by Dr. Andrew Maclean of the Australian Equine Behaviour Centre. A horse was held equally distant from two empty buckets. A measure of feed was poured into one of the buckets. When the horse was released immediately he went straight for the feed, but when he was held for 10 seconds before being released, his choice of bucket was completely random. In other words, he did not remember which bucket held the feed; he could not store that sort of information.

This doesn't mean he's stupid—he's just thinking like a horse! However, a horse can remember for years the exact spot where a mountain lion jumped out at him and avoid this place. For him to survive, this information is crucial. By understanding this aspect of the horse, we can construct "questions" that he is mentally able to answer.

What Is a Stubborn Horse?

In all my years of handling horses I've never met a stubborn horse. I get presented with plenty of horses that are labeled "stubborn," but when I ask how this stubbornness manifests itself, it always boils down to one thing: The horse is described as stubborn when he doesn't do what the human wants.

3-Minute Horsemanship is about letting go of labels like this and asking ourselves *why* the horse doesn't want to do what we want. He may:

- Be in pain.
- Be frightened.
- Be tired.
- Not understand.
- Be too interested in something else.

Once you understand why he won't do what you want, you can change the question so that he finds it easier to answer. The "stubborn" horse then disappears and you are faced with a willing partner. By presenting the horse with a task that has a simple yes-or-no answer, he will move on more quickly because that's how his brain is wired. If he says "No," you can quickly adjust the question so that he is able to say "Yes" instead. And, when you reward him for his "Yes," he will feel encouraged to try again.

This is problem-solving in *micro* parts that altogether "layer" up to a bigger picture. Let's choose an example of a problem that many of us have encountered in our life around horses: an unwillingness to walk through water.

The first thing we need to do is ask ourselves why the horse won't do it. Remember being "stubborn" is not one of the options. So, is he in pain, frightened, tired, not understanding, or too interested in the grass beside the water to just answer our request to walk through?

The most common reason why horses do not willingly walk through water is fear. He has looked at the water and asked himself, "Is this water safe?" And his answer is "No." It is no more complicated than that. So what we need to do is convince him that it *is* safe. This book is all about how to phrase your questions so that the horse says "Yes," as well as telling you what you can do when he says "No."

How Does the Horse Say "Yes" or "No"?

So what does a horse look and feel like when he says "Yes"?

He feels relaxed and soft in his body. In other words, his joints are moving freely and his muscles feel soft to the touch. He is attentive to the person asking the question and looks keen to do more for her.

The horse that says "No," is tense in his body; he walks in a jerky manner and his body will feel hard and unyielding. His attention is elsewhere, normally looking for a means of escape. That may not always be flight; he may freeze, faint (lie down) or fight (bite, strike or kick). Don't be lulled into a false sense of security that a horse is feeling all right about what you are doing because he's standing still. He may just be too afraid to move! Get to know your horse. How does he say "No"?

You need to know how to turn the horse's answer from a "No" into a "Yes." And, remember, his answer will never be "Maybe."

How You Ask the Question

How you ask the horse the question is the key to success. The question, which should ask for one thing only, should elicit a "Yes" or a "No" answer. Let me give you examples:

1 Here is a *simple* question asking for a simple "Yes" or "No": "Can you put your right front foot onto the trailer ramp?"
2 Here is a *complex* question with too many possible answers: "Can you walk into the trailer and stand still?"

If the horse could think like a human he might say, "Well I can put my front feet on the ramp so that's a yes. But, no, I don't like the roof of the trailer so close to my ears. Yes, I do like the hay net, but no, I don't like the horse you want me to travel with. So I'm not going in."

This horse would probably be called "stubborn" because we are thinking he's like a human, with human thought processes. But he cannot think like a human. He is a horse! I really want you to grasp this concept before I move on. The horse is not out to "get one over on you." He doesn't understand the concept of winning. He can say "Yes" or "No" but *never* "Maybe"!

Saying Yes When Your Horse Says "Yes"

The answer the horse gives to your request is never wrong or bad, it's just feedback. He can only answer your question using the information you give him. When students at school are told off for answering a question incorrectly they soon stop answering altogether in case they get it wrong. In extreme cases, they will become completely silent and still; in other words, they freeze up.

So, when the horse says "No" it's because you asked him in such a way that he felt he needed to say "No."

It is your responsibility to ask him in such a way that he wants to say "Yes." However, when a horse doesn't give you the answer you want, just ignore it. Ask the same question again, or rephrase it, so that he feels he can give you a "Yes."

Then you can reward him by saying "Yes," too!

How You Say "Yes" to the Horse.

What motivates him to answer "Yes"? Find out what works for your horse.

There are four ways of letting the horse know that he's giving you the answer you need. The one you use depends on what works for both of you.

1 The most powerful way is to take the pressure off, give the horse peace, and stop asking the question. This is how horses say "Yes" to each other. However humans have other rewards at their disposal that can work equally well if used appropriately.
2 Food given to reinforce behavior can be enormously powerful, but the timing must be spot on

or unwanted behaviors such as barging and biting may appear.
3 Stroking or scratching a horse can be pleasant for him, but it must be remembered that not all horses see being touched as a pleasant experience.
4 Voicing our approval of the horse's correct answer is very common as humans naturally use this with each other. The tone of voice is more important than the words, but horses can learn that "Yes" means "You're doing fine," and "No" means "You're not"!

The timing of any of these responses must be as soon as possible after the answer has been given. Research suggests that it must be within *three* seconds to be effective.

How "Big" Is the Horse's Answer?

The way in which a horse says "Yes" may be tiny or huge. When a horse is starting to go into a trailer he may tentatively place his foot or he may stamp it on the ramp.

When the question is, "Can you put your foot on the ramp?" and he says "Yes," it may be a big bold "Yes" or a tentative quiet "Yes," but it's still a "Yes," so take it!

When a horse says "No," it can also be small or big. A big "No" can be pretty scary: a bolt away from the handler, for example. A small "No" can be a look over his shoulder checking out his escape route. The horse always gives a small "No" before it becomes a big "No," so you need to be observant and notice what's about to happen—then deal with it *before* it happens. This is where *3-Minute Horsemanship* comes in and works so well: you never ask a question where the answers may be bigger than you can handle.

So now that you know what the answer looks like, you can start thinking about some questions. However, before you do, there are some rules that need to be observed—whatever happens. These are "The Seven Basic Principles of *3-Minute Horsemanship*."

THE SEVEN BASIC PRINCIPLES OF *3-MINUTE HORSEMANSHIP*

Some things never change and the *Seven Basic Principles of 3-Minute Horsemanship* are certainly some of them. Basic principles are what you can always fall back on when things get too complicated. So often people ask me how they will know if their training is working or making things worse. I always answer that as long as they have stuck to the Seven Basic Principles no harm will have been done, even if they didn't get the answer they were looking for. These principles form the foundations that must be in place before any horsemanship skills can develop. Seeing as they are basic principles they are presented in no particular order: none of them is of greater importance than another.

- Use the Power of the Pause
- Allow the Horse to Seek Peace
- Know What Success Means
- Respect Personal Space
- Be Consistent
- Never Be Afraid to Start Again
- Be Positive and Believe

Use the Power of the Pause

We live in an instant world. When we press a button we expect an immediate response. We order on the internet and want a delivery the next day. We ask a question and expect an instant answer. But let's think about this "instant" bit.

When we are asked a question what happens? We hear the question, we decide what answer is appropriate, then we answer the question. That's not instant!

The same thing happens with the horse. First of all he needs to recognise that we are asking him to do something, then he needs to decide on the answer, then he replies.

Whenever you ask a question of the horse, you must make sure that he can hear you, that he understands the question and is capable of answering it. Then, just *wait*.

Wait and wait and wait some more!

The question may be as simple as: "Can you walk through this narrow gap?"

Or, you may be cantering around the arena on your horse, and ask him, "Could you please look into the center of the arena very slightly?"

In both cases, you've asked a question. Now let the horse answer it. Don't meddle with him, he's thinking! If you've asked the question correctly, it'll never take him longer than three minutes to give you the answer. That's the *power of the pause.*

Allow the Horse to Seek Peace

When a filmmaker makes a documentary about horses he knows he would soon lose his audience if he filmed just an ordinary day. There would be a lot of eating, a few hours of standing together snoozing, a bit of mutual grooming and rolling, with a few seconds of kicking, chasing and general liveliness thrown in.

Filmmakers sit for months to create a program that is 30 minutes long, and they aren't going to waste all

those exciting seconds of galloping, rearing and chasing by leaving them on the cutting room floor!

So everyone thinks horses spend all their time dashing about. Horses need to eat for 18 hours a day and they certainly don't waste energy galloping around anymore than they have to. Like most of us, they want an easy life, good food, companionship, and freedom from pain and fear.

However, often, when we set about training the horse, we unwittingly put him into very stressful situations where he is unable to express his desire to run away. When a horse is afraid, his learning ability is diminished because all he can think about is leaving. If we slowed down the training process and worked quietly on tasks that the horse is capable of achieving, and rewarding him when he gets it right, he would be more enthusiastic about joining us in the training area every day.

I do believe it goes one stage further, however. I believe horses actively seek peaceful people.

A friend of mine was escorting a ride in Hyde Park in London when one of the riders fell off and the horse bolted. Everyone began running around, trying to catch the frightened horse before he ended up on the heavily trafficked road. He became more and more scared until he saw a young girl sitting quietly on a bench reading a book. She was the only peaceful person he could see in the whole park, so he galloped over and stood with her until help arrived.

Be the peace your horse seeks, and he will always want to be with you.

Know What Success Means

Success is relative. For one person, success is going for a quiet, enjoyable ride, for another it's winning a gold medal.

To be successful you need to know what your goal is, and how you are going to get there. This is the essence of *3-Minute Horsemanship.*

So make a plan that is easy to follow with "mini successes" along the way. By keeping your training sessions short and productive, you will become very aware of the small things that indicate you are moving forward, and therefore feel encouraged to keep going.

The same applies to your horse! Get good at reading him so that you can let him know immediately when he's on the right track. Leave him alone when he's trying, but learn when he needs you to rephrase the question. Even if he just tries to answer and it isn't quite what you were looking for, that is a moment of success because he's trying to work *with* you to find the solution. With a little more information from you, he can get the answer. What a great team!

As a horseman it doesn't matter what milestone you've reached on the way to the top, you will always want to have a willing, relaxed horse because this indicates that he is working with you. When he isn't, you can only ever be the best of the worst on the day.

Respect Personal Space

Everyone has a space around them they call their own. Horses have a personal space too, and if you look at a herd grazing you will often find that there is a regular distance between each individual.

Horses and humans are very particular about whom they let into that personal space, but so often humans treat horses like vehicles and go barging in without checking with the horse first.

Haven't you seen a horse leaning over a gate or door having a quick snooze when along comes a human, gives him a jovial slap on the neck, or starts playing with his lips? Then humans wonder why horses bite or threaten them, or simply move away.

Respect your horse's personal space and he'll respect yours. Never enter into it without offering your hand first, or calling his name. Likewise don't allow him to come into your personal space without him asking first.

When a horse does push into you, do not move away because he will view this as an invitation to get even closer. Always think about *you moving* the horse rather than the horse *moving you*. Back him away from you if he starts pushing into you. For more about personal space, look at the *3-Minute Horsemanship* Ground Exercises, on pp. 12 and 14.

Be Consistent

Being consistent means that each question you ask the horse can only have one correct answer. So when you ask the question, you need to know exactly when you get the answer you want so you can let the horse know!

Whenever you ask him a question, expect an answer, and don't give up until you get the answer or some attempt at it. Horses are so used to humans telling them to do something but giving up before the horse has had a chance to give it a try, they just stop bothering. If we would only wait three minutes, it would save so much wasted training time.

However, sometimes you will think you're asking one question and the horse will think you are asking another. You need to make sure you are clear and consistent in how you ask a question. And, it's really important to let the horse know when he's got it right.

Basically, you are changing your demeanor from expectancy as you wait for the horse to answer correctly, to peaceful relief when he does. Then you can stop asking the question, which is the horse's reward. However, you may need to make this even more obvious for some horses and offer a treat, a stroke or kind word. Find out what makes your horse want to try even harder.

Although I am talking about consistency there are times when you do need to *change* the question because the horse just doesn't understand. Experience will tell you when and how to do this. The beauty of working in three-minute slots is that if it all goes wrong, the consequences are tiny and easily undone.

Never Be Afraid to Start Again

There is a myth that horses are constantly trying to outwit their handlers and are spending their free time just plotting and scheming. Horses just can't think like that.

No matter how long you've been around horses there are always times when nothing seems to be working. No matter what you try the horse isn't giving you anything near the answer you want. You feel yourself becoming irritated, cross, even angry and bad tempered.

STOP! Count to 10, walk away, do whatever defuses a situation that will only end in tears. Getting angry around horses never works and always makes things worse. Once you start putting yourself under pressure then the only individual who will suffer is the horse. Yes, your pride may be a little dented, but the horse may carry the emotional scars of your egotistical outburst forever.

There is no such thing as failure in horsemanship if you know when to stop. It's better to have a go at something and not achieve it than it is to do nothing at all because you can learn through these experiences. Keeping the attempt small means nothing serious will come of it when you don't get the answer you were looking for. Rethink the question to try something different, or go back to doing a movement that he did well.

Be Positive and Believe

If you prepare and understand the route you're going to follow to achieve your task, then believing you'll get there comes easily. When the task looks too big then the steps you've planned are too big, and you need to break them down into easier exercises.

Knowing that you will achieve the final goal—no matter how long it takes or how simple the steps—gives you a positive, confident attitude that reassures the horse you are worth working with. You prove to him that you know what you're doing and can achieve a positive result every day. This is the beauty of *3-Minute Horsemanship.*

It was Bill Dorrance who said, "It's really quite amazing what the horse will do if only he understands what you want. It's also quite amazing what he'll do if he doesn't." So after each training session ask yourself the following questions. If you can answer yes to each one then you've done well. If not, review your strategy and approach the session from another angle next time.

- Did I start the session knowing what I was looking for?
- Did I phrase my question clearly enough for the horse to understand?
- Did I give the horse time to answer?

- Did I stop and reward when the horse was relaxed and willing?
- Did we both respect each other's personal space?
- Did I remain calm throughout the training session?
- Did we both start and finish on a peaceful note?

NOTE TO THE READER

A word about the photographs: In many of them, I am exaggerating my hand, leg and body movements to illustrate a point within the text.

PART ONE

ON THE GROUND

Exercises 1–35

WHY WORK ON THE GROUND WHEN YOU CAN RIDE INSTEAD?

The relationship between horse and human always starts on the ground. If a foal has been born in the wild it might be some time before he actually gets to meet a human but, when he does, it is a pivotal moment for the horse if he is to become a domestic animal.

It is this first meeting that sets the seed for future relationships with people. When it is traumatic, he will always have a feeling of fear around humans. This trauma may be as simple as a halter being put onto his head roughly to being hot-branded and gelded all on the same day.

But one thing's for certain, whether this foal is raised in the wild or domestically, by the time he is a two-year-old, all his human handling will have been from the ground—whether good or bad.

Before you attempt to ride this horse, you need to decide how much he trusts people. The following 35 *3-Minute Ground Exercises* will help you show your horse that being with you is a safe place. This will encourage him to work *with* you, not *for* you. In return, you will feel safer and more confident working with him on the ground and this will lead to better horsemanship skills in the saddle.

What you can do on the ground: Here I am asking my horse to step sideways by touching her side where the girth will be. My hand controls her head, preventing her from stepping forward or backward. This will translate into the aids I give from the saddle later on (see photo on p. 81).

GROUND EXERCISE

1

REQUIREMENTS
None

Horses seek quiet thoughtful people. Agitated or angry people unsettle them and make them difficult to communicate with.

HELPFUL HINT

If you are not comfortable being in the same space as the horse, stand on the other side of the door, gate or fence (fig. C).

Being Still Around a Horse

WHY DO THIS?

Most of us are so busy planning the future we don't give the horse our undivided attention. This exercise helps to prepare your mind to start communication and will help you train your mind to be totally aware of your horse.

HOW TO DO IT

1 Go to the place where your horse appears most relaxed and comfortable. It can be his paddock or his stall as long as he is free to move around normally just as he would if you were not there.
2 Stand or sit with your horse for three minutes (fig. A).
3 Empty your mind. I know how hard this is! But just try to push all those nagging thoughts aside.
4 Ignore the horse. All you are doing is sharing the space. You are not there for any other reason.
5 Be aware of your breathing. Do not change it.
6 Be aware of your heartbeat. Do not change it.
7 If you carry out these instructions, within three minutes, a peace will descend upon you and your horse.

HOW YOU KNOW WHEN YOU'VE DONE IT

• The horse may sigh or yawn (fig. B).
• You will be more aware of sounds around you.
• You will feel peaceful.

WHAT YOU CAN DO IF IT DOESN'T HAPPEN

Your mind is too active is the usual reason, taking your attention away from the present. If you think there is a thought that is stopping you from staying still, write it down on a piece of paper, put it in your pocket and think about it later.

OTHER THINGS YOU CAN DO WITH THIS EXERCISE

Horsemanship is a way of life. You can practice being still anywhere. In the line at the supermarket, waiting at a stop light, or waiting for water to boil are everyday occurrences that help you become patient.

A. *Just being with a horse can be very relaxing and enjoyable.*

B. *Your horse may yawn when you just stand still with him.*

C. *You may want to stand on the other side of the door for safety.*

REQUIREMENTS
None

When a horse's personal space is invaded he may try to defend it.

Measure a Horse's Personal Space

WHY DO THIS?

Human beings have an area around them into which they only allow certain people. This is true for horses, too: They have a personal space that they only let specific horses enter into (fig. A). The size of this area varies enormously from horse to horse, and it changes with the weather, location and circumstances.

When a horse's personal space is invaded his behavior can change. He may become tense, look away or rock his weight back. He may even defend his space by trying to drive the uninvited horse away. If this doesn't work, he will move away to recreate his personal space and distance again. If you can learn to tell when a horse feels uncomfortable, you can begin to develop strategies to help him be more relaxed in your presence. By the time he is running away across the pasture, it's too late to do anything about it!

HOW TO DO IT

1. Go to the place where your horse appears most relaxed and comfortable. Whether paddock or stall, he must be able to move around normally as if you were not there.
2. As you approach the horse look carefully for any indication, however small, that he is not happy about you getting nearer to him.
3. Stop moving, look away and just wait.
4. Within three minutes your horse will acknowledge you by looking at you, flicking an ear toward you, or maybe just relaxing slightly in your direction.
5. Go away.
6. Repeat this exercise every day and one day, the horse's behavior will not change when you approach. He may even come over to meet you. You can repeat this exercise on the same day with some horses, but when they are very "shy," you will have to build this up more slowly.

HOW DO YOU KNOW WHEN YOU'VE DONE IT?

The horse will look relaxed and comfortable as you approach without any indication that he is thinking of leaving.

WHAT YOU CAN DO IF IT DOESN'T HAPPEN

Your horse may already be comfortable with your approach and come to meet you, but some horses have been taught by rough handling that people are not always to be trusted. This exercise may take weeks, months, or even years to reach its conclusion, but will always be successful within three minutes if you look for the slightest improvement every day.

OTHER THINGS YOU CAN DO WITH THIS EXERCISE

Approach the horse holding a "scary" item such as a saddle or a flag, for example.

A. *Horses and ponies often graze close together but with a regular amount of space, like this, between them.*

REQUIREMENTS
None

When you feel confident and brave your horse is more likely to be relaxed because you have given him no reason to look for danger.

Calculate Your Own Personal Space

WHY DO THIS?
It is very easy to pretend to another human being that you are not afraid, but a horse knows as soon as he meets you whether you are scared or not. He may well look for the reason and become anxious, his adrenaline level rising as he decides whether he needs to run away. When you approach a horse, is there a moment when you feel uncomfortable or unsure? This exercise will give you some ideas for becoming more confident when around horses.

HOW TO DO IT
1 Go to the place where he appears most relaxed and comfortable, and where you feel safe and are able to move away freely. This can be the horse's paddock or stall.
2 As you approach the horse be aware of even the tiniest hint or feeling telling you that you are not quite sure about your safety. It might be a dry mouth, shallow breathing, or a few butterflies in your stomach.
3 Stop your approach, look away and just wait.
4 Within three minutes you will feel more relaxed.
5 Go away.
6 By repeating this exercise every day, you will begin to realize that you are getting closer to the horse without feeling afraid of him.

HOW DO YOU KNOW WHEN YOU'VE DONE IT?
Going toward and being close to a horse is no different from going up to shake hands with a good friend (see Exercise 4, p. 16)

WHAT YOU CAN DO IF IT DOESN'T HAPPEN
If you do not feel relaxed and comfortable within three minutes, then you've gone too fast. The power in this exercise comes from stopping the second you feel afraid, not when you feel really scared and want to run away.

OTHER THINGS YOU CAN DO WITH THIS EXERCISE
Do you have any other phobias? It works with a fear of spiders and heights, too!

A. *Ask a friend to come along to give you confidence when you are afraid of getting too close to your horse.*

GROUND EXERCISE

4

REQUIREMENTS
None

Go into the horse's personal space to say "Hello" and receive an acknowledgment in return.

HELPFUL HINT

If you have a horse that has been fed a lot of treats from the hand, he may try to nip you. Ignore this! He must learn the difference between a "handshake" and the offer of a treat.

Shake Hands

WHY DO THIS?

This simple exercise is actually extremely powerful for both horse and handler. When people shake hands, they offer each other their right hand, clasp and shake. A horse uses his head to do this. Watch two horses meeting, nose to nose, as they introduce themselves, thus ensuring that they each have the other's permission to reach into his personal space. We are not going to use our noses as some horses can nip in play, we are going to use our hand.

HOW TO DO IT

1 Have your horse in a halter with a lead rope.
2 Hold your open hand up to the horse's forehead but do not touch him. Your hand should remain about 12 inches (30cm) away from his head. Wait (fig. A).
3 Do not touch the horse. You are offering the handshake and he needs to offer his face in order to return it.
4 Some horses immediately look away, refusing to acknowledge the hand. Wait for the horse to turn his head and brush your hand. Drop your hand and relax.
5 Repeat until the horse is comfortable touching your offered hand. Remember, the horse is touching your hand—you are not touching the horse.

HOW DO YOU KNOW WHEN YOU'VE DONE IT?

The horse will touch your offered hand with his face whenever you ask him. I like my horses to put their forehead onto my hand rather than their mouth (fig. B). This is a personal choice because I like the horse's poll and neck to be low and relaxed as we do this. When his head is raised it can be as a result of tension, or even cause tension.

WHAT YOU CAN DO IF IT DOESN'T HAPPEN

You are *offering* the hand for him to "shake" it. This cannot be forced so don't be tempted to put your hand onto his face. This would be like a person *forcing* another to shake hands by grabbing at him. You must be prepared to wait (fig. C).

OTHER THINGS YOU CAN DO WITH THIS EXERCISE

This powerful exercise stands alone.

A. Offer your hand and wait for the horse to touch it.

B. Your horse will become used to "shaking" your hand, and rest his forehead on it when you offer it.

C. Don't force your horse if he doesn't want to shake hands. Just wait.

5

REQUIREMENTS
None

Teach the horse to listen to you, especially when there's a lot going on. Train him to consistently respond to a special signal to pay attention even when he's distracted.

HELPFUL HINT

Once you have the horse's attention, stop asking for it!

Get a Horse's Attention

WHY DO THIS?
It is impossible to communicate with people when they are not listening to you! Similarly, it is very difficult when there are things distracting your horse when you want to work with him. You could possibly remove them all, but in the long run, this is just a "management" solution rather than dealing with the lack-of-attention issue. And, at a horse show it would be very difficult—actually impossible—to ask everyone at the showgrounds to stop while you compete. So it's much better to teach the horse to listen to you when there's a lot going on.

HOW TO DO IT
1 Practice this at home first. You need to learn how to do this when there are very few distractions around, and build up to a local show level later on.
2 Decide what signal you are going to use that means, "Listen to me, I need your attention!" You can call the horse's name, cluck your tongue, or rattle a few pebbles in a tin can (fig. A). Do not pull on the lead rope because some horses may feel they are under pressure and become "claustrophobic" as a result (fig. B).
3 As soon as you feel that the horse has lost "contact" with you, give him the signal to tell him to give you his attention. Make that signal small at first.
4 Build up the "volume" until the horse looks at you or flicks his ear in your direction.
5 Stop asking as soon as you feel he has acknowledged you (fig. C). This never takes anything near three minutes, so be observant for the smallest signals.

HOW DO YOU KNOW WHEN YOU'VE DONE IT?
The horse will respond to your signal whenever you ask.

WHAT YOU CAN DO IF IT DOESN'T HAPPEN
Every time, make sure you give the *same* signal that only means, "Give me your attention please."

OTHER THINGS YOU CAN DO WITH THIS EXERCISE
You will find this very useful if your horse is distracted at shows or at other busy places. If your training is solid and you have trained him consistently to respond to your signal to pay attention, then bringing his attention back after losing it should be easier.

A. You can rattle a can of pebbles to get your horse's attention.

B. DO NOT pull on a lead rope to get your horse's attention.

C. As soon as he looks at you, stop rattling the can and lean back.

6

REQUIREMENTS
None

If the horse starts "jumping about," you can ask him to move away from your body for your safety.

HELPFUL HINT

This method of backing up your horse is the only safe way to create a space between you and the horse. Remember the reason the horse is going backward, and *not* you, is because when you back away from him he may see that as an invitation to come closer to you.

Back Up Away from You

WHY DO THIS?

When a horse gets overactive while he is close to you, the situation becomes dangerous. So teach your horse to move away whenever you ask, then if he does start jumping about, you are not without a tool to help you. You may need a longer lead rope than usual for this so that the horse can be moved to a safe distance.

The method I am going to show you will help you move an overactive horse away from you without you having to get close to him. It is important that you *do not* move backward away from him because he may see this as an invitation to push into you.

HOW TO DO IT

1 Experiment first to find out what the horse already knows about backing up. Does he back up when you press on his chest, by putting pressure on the lead rope under his nose, or by wriggling the lead rope? Once you know this you can continue as you will need this information later (figs. A–D).
2 Stand in front of your horse, facing him.
3 Move him away from you so that he is about an arm's length away. Notice you move the horse, *not* yourself!
4 Lean in the direction you want him to go. In this exercise, this means you will be leaning toward the horse.
5 Ensure the rope is loose enough so that when the horse moves back he does not have to pull on the rope to do so.
6 Tap the rope with your finger; you will see the vibration travel along the lead rope to the horse's head.
7 Increase the activity along the lead rope until the horse moves back.

HOW DO YOU KNOW WHEN YOU'VE DONE IT?

The horse will respond to the tap on the rope by taking a step back away from you.

WHAT YOU CAN DO IF IT DOESN'T HAPPEN

Increase the pressure of the tap until it becomes a regular thump on the rope. Rhythm is the key here. If the horse has still not moved after 30 seconds, change the question and use the method he already knows to back him away. This may mean putting pressure on the lead rope or pressing on his chest.

As soon as he takes a step back, stop and reward him. Now start again at the very beginning by tapping the rope, slowly building the pressure and repeating everything just as before until you get a step back. As you repeat this he will begin to connect the tap on the rope with backing up, and you will not have to use the method he was previously used to.

OTHER THINGS YOU CAN DO WITH THIS EXERCISE

Back your horse out of the trailer and through narrow gaps.

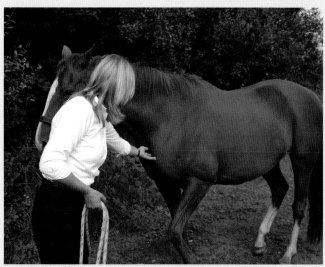

A. *You can touch the horse's chest to ask him to go back . . .*

B. *. . . or, put a little pressure into the rope under his chin . . .*

C. *. . . or, tap on the rope from a distance.*

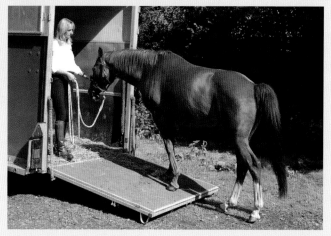

D. *It is easy to unload your horse out of a trailer when he knows how to back up in hand like this.*

GROUND EXERCISE

7

REQUIREMENTS
Exercise 1: Being Still Around a Horse

It's frequently a matter of safety that your horse will stand still when asked.

HELPFUL HINT

This is not a battle of wills or bid for dominance; it's a simple matter of safety that when you need a horse to stand still he does as you ask. "Getting a stop" when you need it could be the difference between life and death!

Teach Standing Still

WHY DO THIS?
The most important "gait" is halt. Any time you need to ask the horse to stand still and wait for the next instruction, he should do so.

HOW TO DO IT
The first thing you need to do is ensure *you* are still and not agitating the horse by being agitated inside yourself!

1 Have your horse on a halter and lead rope.
2 Decide what cue or signal means "Stand still." It could be a vocal one such as "Wait" or "Stand," or a hand signal. Remember the signal you choose must *only* mean "Stand still," never anything else.
3 Ask your horse to stand still using the chosen signal.
4 If he moves, ask again. You are looking for the slightest halt in his movement—the slightest suggestion that he has understood you want him to stand still. Make sure he is not pushing into you.
5 Reward him for standing still *while* he is standing still, not when he has moved off afterward!
6 Initially, do not expect your horse to stand still for long periods. Three minutes may be too long. Look for him to understand that your signal means stand still, and reward him when he gives you the correct response—even if it is only for one second.

HOW DO YOU KNOW WHEN YOU'VE DONE IT?
The horse stands still as soon as you give the signal (figs. A–C).

WHAT YOU CAN DO IF IT DOESN'T HAPPEN
• If the horse keeps on moving, repeat your signal slowly and deliberately. At some point over the next three minutes he will hesitate and stand still. This is where your timing comes in. Be vigilant. Look for that moment when his feet are quiet and let him know that's what you want.
• When it really is still a struggle for him, see if it is the training area that is upsetting him and move him to a place where he feels calmer. Remember, some horses find it difficult to keep their feet still when they are afraid.

OTHER THINGS YOU CAN DO WITH THIS EXERCISE
This exercise is useful in places where everyone around you is very busy, even agitated, and it helps the horse realize that "with you" is a calm place to be.

22 | 3-Minute Horsemanship

A. *You can practice standing still in the pasture . . .*

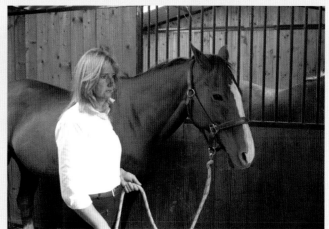

B. *. . . in a stall . . .*

C. *. . . and among other horses.*

REQUIREMENTS

Exercise 6: Back Up Away from You

The horse needs to learn a cue that always means "Go backward."

Back Up a Horse While Beside Him

WHY DO THIS?

It may not always be convenient to be in front of the horse when you back him up. Sometimes you may need to be beside him—or even *behind* him—when you are asking him to come out of a trailer, for example.

HOW TO DO IT

1 First find out what the horse already knows about backing up. Does he back up from you pressing on his chest; by your putting pressure on the lead rope under his nose; or when you wriggle the rope? Once you know this, you can continue because you will need this information later.
2 Stand *beside* your horse facing in the same direction.
3 Lean in the direction you want him to go. In this exercise this means you will be leaning backward.
4 Ensure the rope is loose enough so that when the horse moves back he does not have to pull on the rope to do so.
5 Tap the rope with your finger: you will see the vibration travel along the lead rope to the horse's head (fig. A).
6 Increase the activity on the rope if you have to. As soon as the horse takes a step back, stop asking and reward him.

HOW DO YOU KNOW WHEN YOU'VE DONE IT?

The horse takes a step back when you lean backward and gently tap the rope.

WHAT YOU CAN DO IF IT DOESN'T HAPPEN

Increase the pressure of the tap until it becomes a regular thump on the rope. Rhythm is the key here. If the horse has still not moved after 30 seconds, don't keep nagging him. Use the cue or method he already knows to back up, even if you have to reach under his chin or press on his chest. You are teaching him a different signal from what he already knows so it can take some time for him to make the change. Eventually he will back up with just a tap on the rope.

OTHER THINGS YOU CAN DO WITH THIS EXERCISE

Your regular tap on the rope can be made *in the air* above the rope (instead of *on* the rope) so when the horse sees you lean backward and tap the air, he knows you are asking "Go backward." This means that you can use this signal anywhere around your horse and ask him to back up (figs. B–D). When it is safe to do so, you can even stand behind your horse and have him back toward you.

A. *Start by tapping the rope. Notice I am leaning back here.*

B. *Without touching the rope, I tap the air so that the hand movement alone becomes the signal.*

C. *You can back your horse up from anywhere . . .*

D. *. . . but make sure he knows when to stop!*

GROUND EXERCISE

9

REQUIREMENTS

Exercise 5: Get a Horse's Attention

You can "draw" a horse toward you in order to more easily catch him.

HELPFUL HINT

Make sure the horse respects your personal space and doesn't see your invitation to come to you as an opportunity to run you over. If you think the horse is going to do this: stand up, face him, look straight at him, and put your hand up. If he still keeps coming at you make yourself "big" by jumping in the air, or waving your arms to discourage him (fig. E).

Invite a Horse to Walk Toward You

WHY DO THIS?

If you can gain the horse's attention and get him to come to you, you have made him part of the process of being "caught."

HOW TO DO IT

1 First, choose an area where the horse is comfortable. Make sure you have a positive attitude and are kind to the horse when he comes to you.
2 Start with the horse in a halter and lead rope.
3 Get the horse's attention (Exercise 5).
4 Lean away from him and without moving your feet imagine you are drawing him toward you (fig. A). I think about taking hold of a very long whisker and gently pulling on it!
5 If he does not move, create a little friction on the lead rope by pulling it toward you gently (fig. B).
6 If he still doesn't move, try turning away or taking a step backward to help him feel that there is more of a space to move into.
7 Stop asking the moment there is any movement by the horse toward you even if you see him just slightly rocking rather than moving his feet.

HOW DO YOU KNOW WHEN YOU'VE DONE IT?

The horse will walk toward you on a loose rope.

WHAT YOU CAN DO IF IT DOESN'T HAPPEN

• Suppose the horse is "stuck" and will not come to you, even when there is a fair amount of tension in the rope. Remember, if you put too much tension on the rope it will give the horse something to pull against, thus making matters worse.
• Be sure you are not looking directly at the horse. Your eyes can stop a horse because they might look like a predator's eyes in his mind.
• Do not get into a tug-of-war. There are a number of techniques you can try:
  1 Keeping the tension on the lead rope, move around so that you are able to use the end of the lead rope behind the horse's elbow to "drive" him forward (fig. C).
  2 Try keeping a light tension on the lead rope and walking around to the side of the horse to rock him off balance (fig. D).
  3 You will find that once he has moved his feet, he will take one or two steps toward you, then stop again. Don't worry; just repeat the exercise. Always be aware that too much pressure on the lead rope can actually *cause* a horse to "stick" his feet!
  4 The key is to be happy that he has taken one step. Once he has done this just keep repeating the request until he gets the idea.

OTHER THINGS YOU CAN DO WITH THIS EXERCISE

When you get the body language right you can draw a horse toward you without a lead rope when catching him in the field.

A. Lean back and draw the horse toward you.

B. You may need to exaggerate your lean back and put a bit more tension on the lead rope.

C. Change hands on the lead rope and create energy by swinging the end of the lead rope toward the girth area behind the horse's elbow, bumping his side if you need to.

D. Or pull him off balance to one side.

E. If the horse looks as if he's going to run into you, make yourself "bigger."

GROUND EXERCISE

10

REQUIREMENTS
None

Become synchronized:
you and your horse will
both feel more settled
and content.

HELPFUL HINT

When working at speed,
make sure there is safe
distance between you both.

Synchronize Movement

WHY DO THIS?

In nature, horses live in large herds with each individual watching out for the others. They often synchronize their movement so when they run away as a herd, they don't crash into each other. A herd that is quiet and settled is one that is synchronized. You will often see horses face the same direction while grazing, their feet moving forward at the same time, and turning together.

When you are with your horse, it is similar to a two-horse herd. So if you and your horse become synchronized, you will both feel more settled and content with each other.

HOW TO DO IT

1 Lead your horse with a loose rope. The best position for you to be is at your horse's head—not in front of him or back at his shoulder. This is so you and the horse can see each other's feet.

2 Walk normally to start. Do not use the rope to influence the movement other than to keep the horse in the correct position.

3 Change your way of moving. Start to walk in long, giant steps (fig. A). The horse will start to copy you: He'll also walk with long steps. Remember *do not use the rope*! This exercise is about the horse copying you, not being *made* to copy you.

4 Walk in tiny, baby steps, not too fast or the horse will find it too challenging (fig. B). Sometimes, the horse will actually look right down at your feet to see what steps you are doing.

5 Walk high, walk slowly. Trot slowly, trot fast. Experiment. The horse's movement will eventually synchronize with yours.

HOW DO YOU KNOW WHEN YOU'VE DONE IT?

The horse will copy your steps, footfall for footfall. The more you practice this, the better he will become at being a member of your herd.

WHAT YOU CAN DO IF IT DOESN'T HAPPEN

Don't worry. Sometimes it takes a little time for the horse to "read" the human.

OTHER THINGS YOU CAN DO WITH THIS EXERCISE

Horses don't just synchronize their footfalls. They also tune into each other's breathing, heartbeat and adrenaline levels (figs. C & D). Once you've got the walking sorted out, you can start work on these, too.

Sometimes you can start this exercise by synchronizing with your horse by copying his movement then slowly changing the way you move so that he starts to copy you. And, when you start riding your horse, this synchrony will be magnified!

A. You can walk "long"...

B. ... and "short."

C. Horses naturally synchronize their footfalls...

D. ... as well as breathing, heartbeat, and eating!

GROUND EXERCISE

11

REQUIREMENTS
None

Lowering the head
can reduce adrenaline
and heart rate.

Lower the Head

WHY DO THIS?

Being able to lower your horse's head demonstrates that he is relaxed in his poll, neck and withers. A horse that lowers his head comfortably shows trust in the handler.

HOW TO DO IT

1 Stand beside your horse's head and hold the lead rope under his chin.
2 Put a little downward pressure onto the lead rope and wait (fig. A).
  • Either the horse will lower his head, in which case, let go of the rope, and reward (fig. B) . . .
  • . . . or he might pull his head up—or perhaps, not move his head at all. Keep the downward pressure on for two and one-half minutes; do not start getting heavier with the pressure, just wait. If he still hasn't dropped his head, then see below.

HOW DO YOU KNOW WHEN YOU'VE DONE IT?

You will know you have completed the exercise when the horse lowers his head—even just a tiny movement or a *feeling* of a movement. The first time you do this it may be just a suggestion but, if you repeat the exercise every day for a week, very quickly the horse will smoothly and willingly lower his head on request (fig. C).

WHAT YOU CAN DO IF IT DOESN'T HAPPEN

• If the horse throws his head up violently and suddenly, you have asked too hard and too fast. Use less pressure, be very still and wait to feel him give the very slightest lowering of the head. Then release instantly and reward.
• If the horse is still stuck after two and one-half minutes, reach up with your free hand and put a little pressure on the poll (behind the ears) to help him realize that you want him to move his head down.

OTHER THINGS YOU CAN DO WITH THIS EXERCISE

• Use it to lower your horse's adrenaline and heart rate at competitions.
• Put a bridle or halter on your horse while his head is low (fig. D).

A. *Hold the rope, ask and wait.*

B. *Let him know it is safe to drop his head—reward him.*

C. *Will he leave it down there while you stand up?*

D. *Soon you can even put the bridle on from your knees.*

REQUIREMENTS
None

Loosen the horse's
poll and neck.

Bend the Head Around to the Side

WHY DO THIS?

Being able to bend (flex) your horse's head and neck around to the side shows that he is loose in his poll and neck. A horse that can do this comfortably shows that he trusts the handler.

HOW TO DO IT

1 Starting position: Stand beside your horse's shoulder facing forward.
2 Use your outside hand, the one that is farthest away from the horse, to hold the lead rope about 12 inches (30cm) from the clip. As you get better at this exercise, this length will become greater.
3 Use your inside hand, the one nearest the horse, to hold any extra lead rope.
4 Put a little pressure onto the lead rope, and ask the horse to bring his nose around toward you. Wait (fig. A).
   • Either the horse will bring his nose around to you, in which case, release the rope and reward. The movement should feel loose and smooth like a well-oiled hinge.
   • Or the horse may pull his head away or not move his head at all. Keep the pressure but do not get heavier; just wait (fig. B). You must feel for the slightest give—it may be no more than a whisker twitch—then release. When the horse seems to have gone to sleep and is really hanging onto the rope after two and one-half minutes of asking, see below.

HOW DO YOU KNOW WHEN YOU'VE DONE IT?

You will know you have completed the exercise when the horse's nose moves toward you—even a tiny movement—or you get a *feeling* of movement. The first time you do this it may be just a suggestion of movement. If you repeat the exercise every day for a week, very quickly the horse will smoothly and willingly bring his nose around to you on request. He should, one day, be able to bring his nose right around to touch his side whenever you ask him to.

WHAT YOU CAN DO IF IT DOESN'T HAPPEN

• When the horse pulls his head away or throws it upward, you have asked too hard and too fast. Use less pressure, be very still and wait to feel him give the very slightest movement of the nose toward you, then release instantly, and reward.
• If the horse is still stuck after two and one-half minutes, without taking the pressure off, swap the lead rope to your inside hand, which already has the extra lead rope in it. Your outside hand is now free to reach over the horse's nose, around to the other side. Using one finger, gently press the opposite side of his face to encourage him to bring his nose around to you (fig. D). As soon as he does, release instantly.

OTHER THINGS YOU CAN DO WITH THIS EXERCISE

• Use it to lower your horse's adrenaline and heart rate at competitions.
• Put a bridle or halter on your horse knowing that you have his full attention.

A. Hold the rope and ask the horse to bring his nose around.

B. The horse may pull against you; just hold and wait.

C. Sometimes just a small bend is enough for the day.

D. A supporting hand can sometimes help the horse understand what you are asking.

13

REQUIREMENTS

Exercise 12: Bend the Head Around to the Side

The horse that can bend his head to his opposite side from where you are standing is showing his trust in you.

HELPFUL HINT

Be sure your horse knows that he must not step into your personal space (fig. D). If he tries to straighten his neck while his head is bent away, he can step his hindquarters toward you and onto your feet.

Bend the Head Away to the Opposite Side

WHY DO THIS?

Being able to bend (flex) your horse's head and neck around to the opposite side shows that he is loose in his poll and neck. A horse that can do this comfortably shows that he trusts the handler, because he can no longer see the handler.

HOW TO DO IT

1 Starting position: Stand beside your horse with your belly button facing underneath his neck.
2 Use the hand nearest to the horse's head to gently hold the halter just where it touches his lower jaw (fig. A).
3 Use your other hand to hold the lead rope.
4 Put a little pressure onto the halter to ask the horse to bend his nose away from you (figs. B & C).
5 When he flexes away from you, release and reward.

HOW DO YOU KNOW WHEN YOU'VE DONE IT?

The horse will smoothly take his nose away from you toward his opposite shoulder.

WHAT YOU CAN DO IF IT DOESN'T HAPPEN

If it doesn't happen straight away, don't get stronger; just wait. Some horses find this a very difficult exercise because not only are you asking them to take their eye off you, they are also trusting that you are looking out for them on that blind side. Look for the tiniest release, and as soon as the horse loosens up, stop asking. This exercise cannot be forced.

OTHER THINGS YOU CAN DO WITH THIS EXERCISE

This is a great way to test how ready your horse is to work with you. A horse that does not want to bend may be fearful or in pain.

A. *Hold the halter against the lower jaw with the extra rope in your other hand.*

B. *Tip your horse's nose away from you . . .*

C. *. . . and all the way around, if you can.*

D. *If he tries to move his whole body, support him by using your other hand.*

14

Use roping techniques to instill trust.

HELPFUL HINTS

• Practice these rope skills, both left- and right-handed, away from the horse first.

• Do not move on too quickly. Trust lost while swinging a rope over a horse's head will take a long time to regain.

• Do not throw the end of your rope around the horse's head because it could flick into his eye and cause an injury.

Throw a Rope Over the Horse's Head

WHY DO THIS?
Whether or not you are going to start roping cattle, getting your horse used to a rope swinging around his head will build trust into your relationship. Should your reins ever end up over your horse's ears or face, he is far less likely to panic if he has already learned that ropes are not dangerous.

HOW TO DO IT
1 You will need to have a halter and lead rope on your horse. Make sure the rope or lead rein is long enough to give plenty of room for the rope to swing clear of the horse's ears.
2 Hold the lead rein about 2 feet (60 cm) from the clip, and gently throw the other end of the rope along the ground beside the horse (fig. A).
3 Gauge his reaction. Ask yourself whether you need to repeat this until he relaxes, or if you can throw the rope nearer to his feet and legs.
4 Look for relaxation and acceptance.
5 Build up to throwing the end of the rope around the horse's feet and legs, over his back and neck (figs. B & C). Gently throw the rope and be careful it does not hurt the horse.
6 Take the end of the rope and drape it around your horse's head, eyes, and ears. Go carefully. This is a very delicate, vulnerable area. Should you hurt your horse, he will learn not to trust you.
7 Once the horse accepts the end of the rope being draped and dropped all around and over him, you can start to throw the rope over his head. Hold the lead rope so that between 8 feet (2.5m) and 10 feet (3m) is loose between you. Imagine it is a skipping rope between you and your horse's chin. Start to swing it. Keep your body language relaxed.
8 Increase the arc of the swing until the rope swings right over the horse's head, staying clear of his ears (fig. D).
9 You can increase the challenge by swinging the rope from any position around your horse (fig. E).

HOW DO YOU KNOW WHEN YOU'VE DONE IT?
The horse stands still and accepts the rope being swung over his head.

WHAT YOU CAN DO IF IT DOESN'T HAPPEN
Either you've moved on too fast for the horse to accept each stage, or your rope skills need further practice away from the horse.

OTHER THINGS YOU CAN DO WITH THIS EXERCISE
It helps to prepare your horse to accept a rider roping from the saddle. In addition, when riding with one rein, you can throw it over to the other side of the horse without having to pass it under his neck, a maneuver that can unbalance both the rider and the horse.

A. Throw the rope along the ground . . .

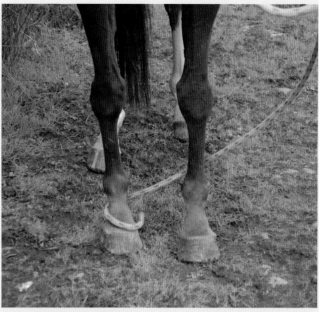

B. . . . around the horse's feet . . .

C. . . . and over the horse's back.

D. Throw the rope over his head from the front . . .

E. . . . from anywhere!

15

REQUIREMENTS
None

This leading exercise demonstrates the horse's independence, balance, and that horse and human are working together.

HELPFUL HINT

Don't get into a tug of war with your horse. He is stronger than you!

Lead with a Loose Rope

WHY DO THIS?

When the lead rope between the handler and horse is loose, it enables the horse to balance himself and maintain a safe distance between himself and the handler, which shows that the horse and human are working together.

HOW TO DO IT

1 Ask the horse to walk with you by leaning forward in the direction you want to go (fig. A). When he doesn't take a step put a little pressure on the lead rope. If he still doesn't walk forward use the end of the rope and tap him behind the shoulder to encourage him (fig. B).
2 As soon as he takes a step, let the rope go loose, and walk with him even if it is for only a few steps. If he stops just repeat the process.
3 When you are consistent, the horse will very soon learn to travel beside you on a loose rope.

HOW DO YOU KNOW WHEN YOU'VE DONE IT?

The horse travels beside you like he is your shadow and as if there is no lead rope attached.

WHAT YOU CAN DO IF IT DOESN'T HAPPEN

• When the horse ends up behind you, do not try to pull him along. Put pressure behind the shoulder by tapping him with the lead rope to encourage him to hurry up.
• When the horse ends up being in front of you, turn away from him and walk in the opposite direction with energy and commitment (fig. C). You'll find that he is no longer in front of you.
• Ask the horse to back up if he continues to walk in front of you (fig. D).

OTHER THINGS YOU CAN DO WITH THIS EXERCISE

This really keeps your horse *with you* without you having to try and use your strength to keep him with you. Eventually, you will not need a lead rope to lead your horse.

A. The horse should walk beside you.

B. If he starts hanging behind, put energy behind his shoulder to ask him to join you.

C. If he walks in front of you, one way to correct him is to turn and walk in the opposite direction.

D. When he starts to lead you, ask him to back up beside you.

GROUND EXERCISE

16

REQUIREMENTS

Exercise 13: Bend the Head
Away to the Opposite Side

When you can easily move the horse's front end over you are preparing him to be light in the bridle when he's being ridden.

HELPFUL HINT

Some horses throw their heads, rather than releasing their shoulders, to take a step. Be careful to stay at a safe distance and keep gently asking, looking for even the tiniest answer that is taking things in the right direction.

Move the Front End Over

WHY DO THIS?

Being able to move the horse's front end, his head and shoulders, easily and softly, not only makes handling him in tight spaces much safer, it also prepares him to be light in the bridle when ridden.

HOW TO DO IT

1 Starting position: Stand beside your horse with your belly button *facing* underneath his neck.
2 Use your hand nearest to the horse's head and gently hold the halter just where it touches his lower jaw (fig. A).
3 Your other hand holds the lead rope.
4 Put a little pressure onto the halter, asking the horse to bend his nose away from you (fig. B).
5 Now lift (increase) your energy level because you want him to start to move his feet.
6 Keep your energy level up and, very slightly, increase the pressure on the halter.
7 The horse should step over with his front feet.
   • Either he will step with the front foot farthest away then follow it with the one nearest you (fig. C) . . .
   • . . . or, he will step over with the front foot nearest you then the farther foot (fig. D). The most important thing is that he does *not* step forward or back. He should keep his hind feet relatively still while the forehand moves around them in a circle—in other words, he's doing a turn on the haunches.

HOW DO YOU KNOW WHEN YOU'VE DONE IT?

The horse's head, shoulders and feet will have moved away from you softly and smoothly, while the hind feet will have just walked on the spot with very little forward or backward movement.

WHAT YOU CAN DO IF IT DOESN'T HAPPEN

• This is a perfect example of a 3-Minute Exercise. Set up the request to step over and wait. To start with you may not get a step, just a rock or a shuffle. Take it! Reward the try. Then ask again. Some horses find this enormously challenging, so give them time to find the answer.
• If the horse pushes forward to avoid stepping over, use your hand that's holding the halter to put a little pressure toward the chest to stop the forward motion.
• Should the horse back up, lift your hand on the halter to stop the backward motion.

OTHER THINGS YOU CAN DO WITH THIS EXERCISE

You can use it to supple your horse's shoulders and neck, and start lateral maneuvers, in hand. For young horses, this is very good preparation for ridden work.

A. *Hold the halter against the lower jaw.*

B. *Ask the horse to bend away so that his nose leads the movement.*

C. *The horse can first step over with the foot that is farthest away . . .*

D. *. . . or he can step his nearest foot over the other one first.*

17

REQUIREMENTS

Exercise 12: Bend the Head Around to the Side

Being able to move the hindquarters easily means you are in control of the horse's "engine."

HELPFUL HINT

Slow down and be very quiet and deliberate in your request.

Move the Hind End Over

WHY DO THIS?

Being able to move your horse's hindquarters over means that he is loose in his hips. When done correctly it shows that the horse has willingly released his whole body to the handler.

HOW TO DO IT

1 Flex your horse's head around toward you so that it feels relaxed and free (fig. A). The horse must keep this bend throughout this exercise. If at any time you lose it, you must get it back before continuing.
2 Your outside hand holds the lead rope, including any of the extra length you are not using. You are relaxed in your body and simply asking the horse to bring his head around to you.
3 With the hand nearest the horse, touch his side about where your leg would be if you were riding him (fig. B).
4 Raise your energy level and turn your body so that you are facing the ribs of the horse (fig. C).
5 With your hand, gently press the hair on his side. If nothing happens:
6 Press the skin. If nothing happens:
7 Press the muscle. If nothing happens:
8 Press the rib.
9 At some point the horse will step his hind end over—the hind foot on your side of the horse will step under his belly away from you (fig. D).
10 Release the pressure of your hand on his side and rub him. Do not remove your hand from his side. Leave it there loosely without any energy in it.

HOW DO YOU KNOW WHEN YOU'VE DONE IT?

You will know when the horse's hind leg steps under his belly moving his rib cage and hind end away from you. If you repeat the exercise every day for a week, the horse will smoothly and willingly step over.

WHAT YOU CAN DO IF IT DOESN'T HAPPEN

• If the horse just doesn't move, wait. If he still hasn't moved after two-and-one-half minutes, curl your fingers in toward your palm to create a cup shape and tap (do not hit or strike) the side of the horse in the same place you have already been asking. This action creates a clapping noise, and the sudden shock is usually enough to cause the horse to step over. Remember it's the noise that causes him to step away, not pain! Make sure you practice this on yourself first. If it hurts then you aren't doing it right.
• When your horse doesn't step under his belly but just shuffles around or steps behind the other hind leg, keep asking until he does.
• What if you get more than one step? You are doing too much. Do less and remember to stop asking him to move as soon as he seems to be about to step. Your aim is to get one step whenever you ask for it; then you can just repeat the question to get as many as you want. Remember, you are not chasing the horse around, you are just asking him to step over with his hind end.

A. *Ask the horse to bend his nose around to you.*

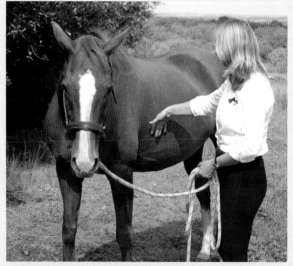

B. *Place the back of your hand on his side.*

C. *Raise your energy level and turn your hand over.*

D. *The horse will step his hind leg under himself.*

OTHER THINGS YOU CAN DO WITH THIS EXERCISE

As a ridden exercise it can save your life as an "emergency stop": When a horse steps under his body with his hind leg in this way, it disengages his "engine" and stops him from running away with you.

REQUIREMENTS

Exercises 16 and 17: Move the Front
End Over and Move the Hind End
Over. Both exercises need to be solid
before you attempt this new one.

Good preparation for
lateral work under saddle.

HELPFUL HINT

Get good at moving each
end of the horse quietly and
smoothly before you start
to put them together to get
him to go sideways.

Move a Horse Sideways

WHY DO THIS?
This is a great exercise for loosening your horse's body and preparing him
for lateral work when being ridden.

HOW TO DO IT
1 Hold the halter on the jaw looking for a soft bend away from you, raise
   your energy level, then ask him to move his feet (figs. A & B).
2 Move the hind end by bending him toward you, putting your hand on
   his side on the ribs, raising your energy level, and asking him to step his
   hind end over (fig. C).
3 Now repeat the above but with less time between Steps 1 and 2. Stop
   and reward often: Even just one step needs lots of praise.
4 The forehand will move over followed by the hind end until the horse
   appears to be traveling sideways.

HOW DO YOU KNOW WHEN YOU'VE DONE IT?
The horse will smoothly move sideways away from you as if gliding on rails
with no forward or backward movement.

WHAT YOU CAN DO IF IT DOESN'T HAPPEN
First, go back to getting the front end moving and the back end moving
separately and really smoothly. It's such a good-looking move, we all rush at
doing it before the horse is really ready. Look for one step and make that the
end of your 3-minute session. If you keep on hammering away at it, the horse
will get resentful, which then makes completing this exercise impossible.

OTHER THINGS YOU CAN DO WITH THIS EXERCISE
You can side-pass over logs and barrels, and it helps supple your horse for
riding (fig. D). This exercise prepares your horse for lateral work in the
saddle.

A. *Place one hand on the halter and the other on the horse's side.*

B. *Ask the forehand to step over.*

C. *Ask the hind end to go over.*

D. *Ask for both ends to step over along a log.*

19

REQUIREMENTS

Exercise 6: Back Up Away from You

When a horse will back up regardless of whatever is behind him, it shows that he trusts you.

HELPFUL HINT

Make sure the fence is solid and safe in case the horse runs backward into it.

Back Up to a Fence

WHY DO THIS?

This is an exercise in trust: The horse needs to believe that you have his safety in mind.

HOW TO DO IT

1 Ensure the horse is happy to back up for you—the handler—using a method that makes both comfortable.
2 Choose a fence or any barrier that is solid and safe. Wire or electric fences are not good choices.
3 Position your horse at least 12 feet (4m) from the fence with his hind end toward it (fig. A). Some horses may need a greater distance than this to start with.
4 Back up the horse. Concentrate on the backing up; do not focus on the fence (fig. B).
5 Be aware of the smoothness of the horse's movement.
6 If the horse shows any hesitation, ask for one more step then stop asking and finish the session for the day. He will back up farther tomorrow.

HOW DO YOU KNOW WHEN YOU'VE DONE IT?

If the horse backs right up to the fence with his back end touching it, this exercise is complete.

WHAT YOU CAN DO IF IT DOESN'T HAPPEN

• First, make sure the backing up is smooth in a wide open space, that is, with no fences nearby. Introducing a fence a long way away, as much as 50 feet (15m) may be where you need to start. Back the horse up until you feel him start to hesitate. Ask for one more step, reward and finish for the day. Mark the stopping place so that for the next few days you can see the horse getting closer to the fence each time.
• It is no use getting into a fight with a horse by trying to push him back. Just look for the moment of hesitation then ask for one more step. This gives him confidence that you will not try and force him. Horses that find this exercise difficult are afraid: When you are afraid of something it doesn't make you braver when someone tries to force you.

OTHER THINGS YOU CAN DO WITH THIS EXERCISE

Back your horse into trailers, stables and through gates (fig. C).

A. *Position your horse some distance from the fence.*

B. *Eventually he will trust you enough to back right up to the fence.*

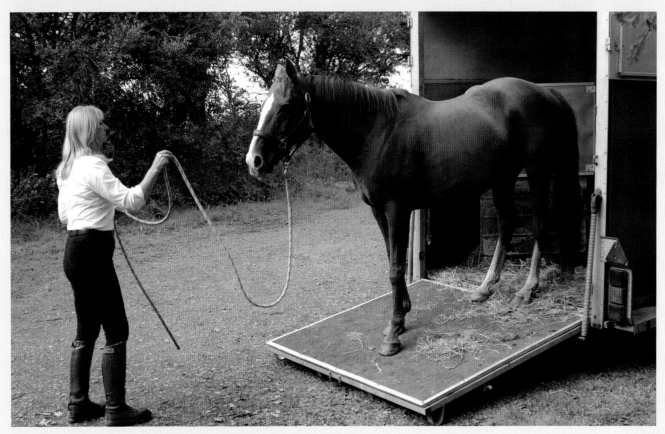

C. *You can try backing your horse into the trailer.*

GROUND EXERCISE

20

REQUIREMENTS

Exercise 15: Lead with a Loose Rope. This helps when the horse finds moving forward difficult when you are on his "other" (off) side.

Lead from the Off Side

WHY DO THIS?

Convention has trained us that we should be doing everything from the *left* side of the horse (the *near* side). The reason behind this tradition is simple: When wearing a sword as most people did on their left side, the near side of the horse was the easiest and safest way for the rider to mount.

The problem with doing everything with the horse from just one side is obvious: The horse, as well as the handler, become one-sided. When you ride the horse you want to be able to ride *both* sides of him, so it seems sensible to work on both sides from the ground.

HOW TO DO IT

1 Approach the horse on the off (right) side. You may need to spend some time on this side of the horse just being still or stroking him. It's surprising how many horses do not like you on their right side (fig. A).
2 Put the halter on from the off side. You may need to adapt your halter to be able to do this (fig. B).
3 Lead your horse from his off side (fig. C).
4 Release your horse from the off side.

HELPFUL HINT

Persevere! It seems very strange at first but the more you do things from the "wrong" side, the more "right" it begins to feel.

HOW DO YOU KNOW WHEN YOU'VE DONE IT?

Once you start working on both sides of the horse, you will start to forget which the "normal" side is. And your horse will begin to feel *straighter* and *more even* under saddle.

WHAT YOU CAN DO IF IT DOESN'T HAPPEN

• It's going to be quite hard to start with when you've spent all your life leading and working horses from the near side, but persevere and you'll soon start to feel differences in your horse.
• Look at Exercise 15: Lead with a Loose Rope, and use the same techniques to help you here.

OTHER THINGS YOU CAN DO WITH THIS EXERCISE

Saddle, blanket, and bridle your horse from the off side, too.

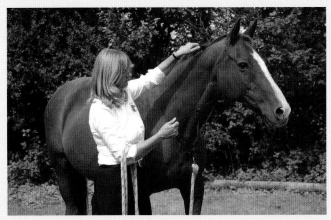

A. *Some horses find bending around on this side quite difficult at the beginning.*

B. *Put on the halter from the off side.*

C. *Leading from the off side requires persistence if you have always done everything from the opposite side of the horse.*

GROUND EXERCISE

21

REQUIREMENTS
None

The horse begins
to notice your body
language and uses
it as cues.

HELPFUL HINT

Rhythm in the movement
really helps here. Count
your steps out loud if you
have to, like the ticking of
a clock.

Walk Forward and Backward a Specific Number of Steps

WHY DO THIS?

We are all lazy when we lead, allowing the horse to drift into a halt not considering the consequences. Then, when we do want the horse to stop in a particular spot and he doesn't, we get angry! It's our inconsistency in our everyday leading that has made this happen.

HOW TO DO IT

1 On a loose rope, lead your horse forward five steps and stop. This isn't six steps or four steps, or even five-and-a-bit! It is *five* steps with the front feet. The front feet are easy to see so that's a good starting point.
2 Right front, left front, right front, left front, right front, STOP!
3 Now ask the horse to back up five steps: right front, left front, right front, left front, right front, STOP.
4 When walking five steps is working, choose to walk six forward and three back, or ten forward and two back. It doesn't matter how many forward or backward steps you do as long as the horse takes the number of steps you planned in advance.

HOW DO YOU KNOW WHEN YOU'VE DONE IT?

The horse walks forward in time with your count, stops, and walks backward in time with your count, then stops. You will feel in synchrony with your horse.

WHAT YOU CAN DO IF IT DOESN'T HAPPEN

The biggest mistake is not preparing the horse for the stop. When you are planning to take *five* steps forward you need to start planning the stop on step number *two*. As with any exercise, prepare the horse for the maneuver.

OTHER THINGS YOU CAN DO WITH THIS EXERCISE

Choose a specific point or mark to walk to, and stop at that point or on the mark (figs. A–C). Become interested in how your horse starts to watch you for subtle body language cues that tell him that you're going to ask him to walk, stop, and back up.

A. *Choosing a marker to walk to will help you be more accurate to start.*

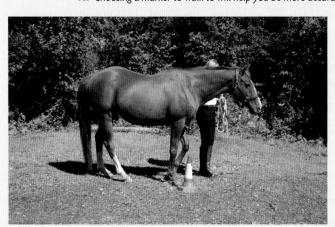

B. *Correct the horse if he goes too far beyond your mark.*

C. *Once you start counting steps you won't need a marker, only honesty!*

22

REQUIREMENTS
None

When a horse has "loose" shoulders he will be "loose" in his feet, too, and therefore much easier to maneuver, whether in hand or being ridden.

HELPFUL HINT

Don't let the horse push you around. If he evades moving the foot by running into you, back him away immediately and ask again.

Free the Shoulders

WHY DO THIS?

Many horses are tight in their shoulders. This can be due to fear—or just a bad habit. When you loosen the shoulders it helps the horse to use his body more efficiently, thus preventing injury and soreness. Many horses become more relaxed and easier to handle when they have completed this exercise.

HOW TO DO IT

1 Stand in front of your horse, facing him.
2 Imagine you are looking in a mirror and the horse is your reflection. When you move you want the horse to copy you.
3 Hold the lead rope, which connects you to the horse, in your right hand.
4 Lift the rope hand up and out to the side, opening your shoulder.
5 To start, the rope will be loose, but as you lift your hand up, the rope becomes a little tighter.
6 You are aiming for the horse to step out and to the side with his left front foot—thus opening his shoulder (fig. A).
7 Repeat for the opposite shoulder (fig. B).

HOW DO YOU KNOW WHEN YOU'VE DONE IT?

The horse will lift his left front foot up off the ground and put it out to the side, or his right, depending on which side you are working with.

WHAT YOU CAN DO IF IT DOESN'T HAPPEN

• At first, your horse may do everything but pick up the foot you want. Keep asking even if you have to walk around to the side and rock the horse off balance.
• If he moves the other foot first, just ignore it and concentrate on the foot you want him to move. As soon as he lifts that foot even an inch or a few centimeters to the side, stop and reward him. You will find one foot is easier to move than the other.
• When the horse steps forward, back him up and ask again.
• Sometimes it helps the horse to back up first before stepping out, because backing up takes the weight off his front end.

OTHER THINGS YOU CAN DO WITH THIS EXERCISE

This is really useful when your horse is heavy in the halter or bridle because the exercise shows him that freeing up his shoulders makes him feel more comfortable.

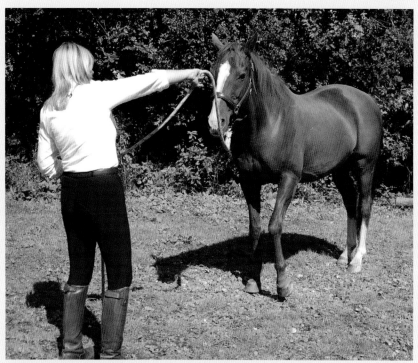

A. *This is freeing up the horse's left front shoulder by moving the left foot.*

B. *To move the other foot, put the rope into your other hand and reverse the directions. I am asking the horse's right shoulder to open by getting him to step out with the right foot.*

GROUND EXERCISE

23

REQUIREMENTS

Exercise 6: Back Up Away from You and Exercise 22: Free the Shoulders

Control the feet and you control the horse.

HELPFUL HINT

Be very clear and deliberate in how you move the rope. If you are "fluffy," the horse just won't know what you are asking.

Place the Front Feet

WHY DO THIS?

If you can exactly place the horse's feet where you want, you are truly in control of your horse.

HOW TO DO IT

1 Hold the rope so it comes out of the bottom of your fist and goes directly to the head of the horse.

2 Face the horse so that he is looking directly toward you.

3 With this rope in your right hand, you are now in communication with the horse's left front foot.

4 Put a little pressure on the rope thus "drawing" the horse's left foot toward you (fig. A). As soon as he starts to bring the left foot forward, stop asking, and he will place it on the ground and leave it there. If he steps again, you did not stop asking soon enough.

5 Now you are going to ask him to put the left foot back where it was (fig. B). Release the rope, rock your weight toward him and put a little rhythmic pressure onto the rope as in Exercise 6 (p. 20). The horse will lift the left foot and put it back where he started.

6 Now ask the horse to step out and place that left foot out to the side. Think of the horse as being a mirror image of you: Lift up your right hand (still holding the rope in it) and move it out to the side; he should lift up his left foot and put it out to the side (see Exercise 22, p. 52).

7 To ask him to put this foot back, put the rope into your left hand and lift it up. This makes him want to step with his *right* leg, but because his *left* leg is out to the side, he will step with that one first, which essentially returns it to the original position.

8 To work with the horse's other foot—the right one—just swap the right and left directions given above.

HOW DO YOU KNOW WHEN YOU'VE DONE IT?

The horse will freely move his foot forward, backward, left and right on request—even onto a specific mark (fig. C).

WHAT YOU CAN DO IF IT DOESN'T HAPPEN

The most common reasons for having trouble with this exercise are:

• You ask too much and get too many steps.

• The rope to the horse's head is too loose: When you start, the horse really needs to feel the pressure of the rope in order to "hear" your request.

• The horse walks forward as you ask for the sideways step—put rhythmic pressure down the lead rope to correct him. In other words, ask him to back up rather than walk forward.

OTHER THINGS YOU CAN DO WITH THIS EXERCISE

When you can place the horse's foot anywhere, you can ask him to put his foot onto a mark on a trailer ramp, a bridge, or into a river (fig. D). This takes the focus off the challenge as he is concentrating on moving his feet.

A. *Moving the horse's left front foot forward.*

B. *Moving the horse's left front foot back.*

C. *Asking the foot to step on a particular mark.*

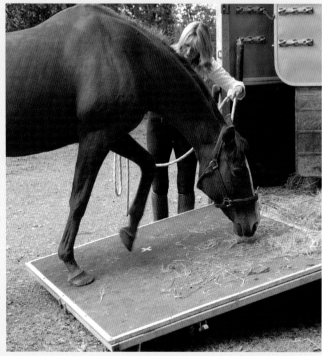

D. *When you put a mark on a trailer ramp (see yellow "x") you can forget about loading the horse and just work on loading the feet!*

24

REQUIREMENTS
None

When you can move your horse's hind feet whenever you want, it becomes easy to step around an obstacle or choose the leading leg as you go into a canter.

HELPFUL HINT

This is a quiet journey of exploration. Be prepared to experiment and play at moving your horse's foot onto a specific mark. When it doesn't work, you've still just learned something!

Place the Hind Feet

WHY DO THIS?
When you can choose exactly where you want the horse to place his feet, you are truly in control.

HOW TO DO IT
1 Hold the rope so it comes out of the bottom of your fist and goes directly to the head of the horse.
2 Face the horse so that he is looking directly toward you.
3 Hold the rope in your right hand. You are now in communication with the horse's *right hind* foot—his *off* hind foot (fig. A).
4 Look down the right side of the horse at the right hind foot; you want this foot to step under the horse's belly. Lift your right hand and push your elbow in toward your body. Start to walk around the horse toward the right hip. The horse is going to activate that hip to step his right foot under his belly (fig. B).
5 Keep walking around toward that hip. If the horse has not stepped underneath by the time you get there, give a sharp push onto the hip so that the horse goes off balance and steps over (fig. C). Even if he doesn't step under his belly, you're starting to show him the sort of answer you are looking for.
6 Repeat this until you find the horse is beginning to step when you lift the rope, push your elbow into your ribs, and look down the side of his body.
7 To ask him to step the foot back to where it started, just swap the right and left directions given above, which causes him to move in the opposite direction.
8 To move the hind foot forward and backward, you need to experiment! Concentrate totally on the foot you want to move and move the rope around until you find whatever position "speaks" to that foot. I find that if I hold the rope as above and lift it up and slightly out to the opposite side, it moves the horse's diagonally opposite hind foot. However, this exercise is so much about feel and trial and error you need to spend time just doing it!

HOW DO YOU KNOW WHEN YOU'VE DONE IT?
The horse will freely move his hind foot forward, backward, right and left on request—even onto a specific mark (fig. D).

WHAT YOU CAN DO IF IT DOESN'T HAPPEN
The most common reasons for having trouble with this exercise are:
• You ask for too much and get too many steps.
• The rope to the horse's head is too loose: When you start, the horse really needs to feel the pressure of the rope in order to "hear" your request.
• The horse walks forward as you ask for the sideways step—put rhythmic pressure down the lead rope to correct him. In other words, ask him to back up rather than walk forward.

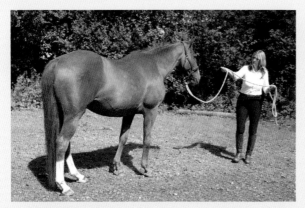

A. *I am "talking" to the horse's hind leg nearest to the camera—the horse's off hind leg.*

B. *Now the foot has stepped under the horse's body.*

C. *When the horse doesn't step under, you may need to push on his hip.*

D. *Experiment by asking your horse to step on a marker.*

E. *The ultimate test: Can you place all four feet on a plank on the ground and ask your horse to walk along it footstep by footstep?*

OTHER THINGS YOU CAN DO WITH THIS EXERCISE

Start to place your horse's feet on specific marks, as in Exercise 23. This helps you forget the challenge of the "obstacle," which often leads to success (fig. E).

GROUND EXERCISE

25

REQUIREMENTS
None

Gives the horse overall confidence and security when crossing strange footing.

HELPFUL HINT

Remain calm and detached. Observe your horse very closely so that you never push him to the point where he feels he needs to run away.

Walk Over Unusual Surfaces

WHY DO THIS?
To encourage your horse to be braver and safer out on the trail.

HOW TO DO IT
1 Start with a tarpaulin, flat board, or other non-slip material on the ground.
2 Lead your horse toward the new surface (fig. A).
3 As soon as you feel him hesitate (if he does), stop (fig. B).
4 Relax.
5 Wait for your horse to relax (fig. C).
6 Lead him away from the surface and repeat Steps 2 through 5 until he walks over the surface (figs. D–F).

HOW DO YOU KNOW WHEN YOU'VE DONE IT?
The horse will lead confidently and on a loose rope over the new footing.

WHAT YOU CAN DO IF IT DOESN'T HAPPEN
You have probably taken the exercise too fast. On Day One, be aware that all you may get from the horse is looking at the strange surface. This may be plenty for him during this session. The horse should never feel so frightened that he needs to leap about or even try to run away.

OTHER THINGS YOU CAN DO WITH THIS EXERCISE
This technique works for trailer loading, going by strange objects when riding out, and crossing water, to name but a few.

A. *Let the horse approach the surface—here, a tarpaulin.*

B. *If the horse becomes concerned, stop; do not pull on him.*

C. *Wait until the horse has relaxed.*

D. *Take the horse away from the tarp.*

E. *Let the horse investigate it.*

F. *Allow him to walk over this new surface.*

GROUND EXERCISE

26

REQUIREMENTS

Exercise 6: Back Up Away from You

Overcome the horse's fear that his feet may not be "safe" thus building trust between you.

HELPFUL HINT

Try not to focus on the pole, lead rope, or line on the ground because this sometimes blocks the horse from moving back: He perceives your interest in the pole and consequently, becomes concerned by it. Instead, look beyond the pole and back him toward that "space."

Back Up Over a Pole

WHY DO THIS?

This is a *trust* exercise as well as one that helps your horse understand where to place his feet safely.

HOW TO DO IT

1   Make sure your horse is very comfortable when backing up. Look for tiny signs of fear or anxiety and help him overcome these, first. You can use any method of backing up for this exercise.

2   Place a pole on level ground so that it can easily be seen—not hidden in long grass. I usually choose a colored pole so that it is very obvious to the horse. If possible use a half-round pole because it won't roll when the horse knocks it.

3   Lead your horse halfway over the pole so that just his front feet are on the other side (fig. A). Some horses do not like standing with a pole under their belly so you may have to work on this first—an extra *3-Minute Exercise*!

4   Once he is comfortable standing over the pole, ask him to back up (fig. B). Be soft and quiet. He may go stiff and start looking down or back. Just wait!

5   Wait until the horse gives you the slightest shift backward. He does not need to step back over the pole at all, at first. Remember, him backing up is the important thing, not the pole. So ignore the pole and just work on backing up your horse.

6   Do not be concerned if the horse knocks the pole. This is a trust exercise, and when he feels comfortable he will loosen up his body and elevate his feet. However, he may not be able to do that at the beginning.

7   Once your horse can step back over the pole with his front feet, lead him over it with all four feet on the other side (fig. C). This means you will be working with the back feet now. For most horses, this is very challenging, so again, concentrate on the backing up. Even if the horse goes crookedly, just keep asking for a straight backup and, just as with the front feet, reward the slightest attempt by the horse to go backward.

HOW DO YOU KNOW WHEN YOU'VE DONE IT?

The horse will walk all the way over the pole and back up over it with all four feet—relaxed and willing.

WHAT YOU CAN DO IF IT DOESN'T HAPPEN

Some horses are really scared of poles on the ground! Do not just ask more firmly; you may need to make things easier for him instead. Start by drawing a line or placing a rope along the ground behind him to find out what it is that is stopping the horse. You will be surprised how many horses will not back up a line or onto a different surface. It's a "survival issue" and when you can overcome the horse's reluctance, it will help to build a trusting relationship between you.

OTHER THINGS YOU CAN DO WITH THIS EXERCISE

You can back into a barn and a stall (fig. D). Also back in and out of a trailer.

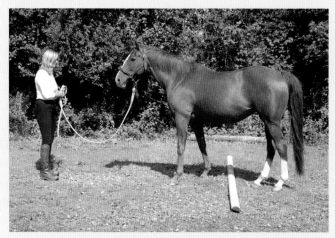

A. *Allow the horse to stand with the pole under his belly.*

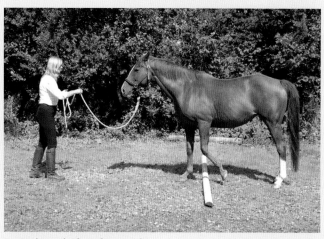

B. *Back just the front feet over first.*

C. *Eventually, you can ask him to back all four feet over.*

D. *Try backing your horse into a stall.*

GROUND EXERCISE

27

Back Up Between Two Poles

WHY DO THIS?

This exercise helps with *straightness,* going both forward and backward. It also accustoms the horse to passing through narrow spaces.

HOW TO DO IT

1 The aim of this exercise is to back the horse in a straight line without touching the poles. The poles can be short or long, set wide apart or very narrow. Start where you and your horse are most comfortable.

2 You can use any method of backing the horse for this exercise, as long as the result is relaxed without resistance.

3 Lead the horse through the poles until his front feet are just beyond the end of the poles (fig. A).

4 Ask him to back up. Go slowly; ask for one step at a time (fig. B).

5 If he goes crookedly you will have to reposition him (see below and fig. C).

6 Keep asking until all four feet are beyond the pole "corridor."

HOW DO YOU KNOW WHEN YOU'VE DONE IT?

The horse will back through the pole corridor without touching the poles.

WHAT YOU CAN DO IF IT DOESN'T HAPPEN

• Start with a short corridor of poles and build up. Look for one straight, willing step and stop there. This is the essence of *3-Minute Horsemanship.*

• If the horse starts to go crookedly, you can straighten him: As his hind end stops backing up straight, turn your horse's head toward the side that is crooked and the horse will step over to become straight again. (I offer more about this in Exercise 33, p. 74.)

• Lead the horse just a few steps into the pole corridor, not all the way, and build up to backing all the way through.

OTHER THINGS YOU CAN DO WITH THIS EXERCISE

Back into a trailer, through a gate, and into a stall.

A. *Start with your horse's feet just beyond the end of the poles.*

B. *Very softly, ask him to back up.*

C. *If he starts to go crookedly you will need to steer him.*

GROUND EXERCISE

28

REQUIREMENTS
Exercise 7: Teach Standing Still

It is useful to encourage your horse to be comfortable next to a fence because you may need to lead him alongside one, or use a fence for mounting.

Stand Next to a Fence

WHY DO THIS?
This can be a real exercise in trust for some horses because many feel vulnerable because their underbelly is next to a hard object that could hurt them. But it is helpful to be able to mount the horse from a fence and have him comfortable enough so you can lead him alongside one.

HOW TO DO IT
1. First, be sure the fence is a safe one. (Barbed wire is always dangerous.) A round pen, gate, or wooden railing are perfect, but use your common sense in this matter as their condition varies.
2. Lead your horse close to the fence—this may be 2 feet (60cm) or 10 feet (3m) away from it (fig. A). You will know if you are too near because the horse will be uncomfortable and may swing his hindquarters away to face the fence.
3. Slowly ask the horse to stand closer to the fence until he is almost touching it (fig. B).

HOW DO YOU KNOW WHEN YOU'VE DONE IT?
The horse will stand quietly and relaxed next to the fence.

WHAT YOU CAN DO IF IT DOESN'T HAPPEN
• Don't assume anything here. It is interesting how many horses find this exercise quite hard, so help your horse by making the fence a good place to be. Hang out, relax, and be comfortable there.
• When your horse keeps moving his hind end away from the fence, you need to immediately reposition him (fig. C). There is no need to tell him off, just put him back where you want him and immediately let him know *that* is what you need. If this still isn't working then you have gone too fast.
• When the horse is afraid of standing so close to the fence, move away until he feels more comfortable, even if it is some distance away. Slowly move him closer and closer to the fence.

OTHER THINGS YOU CAN DO WITH THIS EXERCISE
This prepares your horse to stand next to a vehicle or a mounting block, for example. Or, you can climb the fence so you are higher than the horse when working with a youngster prior ro riding him (fig. D).

A. *Lead your horse to the fence.*

B. *Ask him to stand next to it.*

C. *If he moves away, gently correct him.*

D. *This is good preparation for mounting the young horse. It gets him used to seeing you above him.*

REQUIREMENTS

Exercise 7: Teach Standing Still

Accustom your horse to standing next to any object that will be safe to use as a mounting block.

HELPFUL HINT

Remember to reward the behavior you want. Reward when the horse is standing next to the mounting block, not when he has moved away. However, when he does, ignore his moving away; really let him know that standing next to the block is what you need.

Stand Still at the Mounting Block

WHY DO THIS?

The action of getting up onto a horse puts you in a very vulnerable position because, if the horse moves, it is very easy to overbalance and get hurt in the process. The rule is: The horse must stand still while you get on, *wherever* or *however* that may be. This can be a real exercise in trust for some horses. Many feel vulnerable so close to a hard object that could hurt them; or they have a painful or anxious memory connected with a mounting block.

HOW TO DO IT

1 Ensure the mounting block is a solid mass—not slippery to stand on—and that it doesn't have any sharp edges that could hurt the horse. And, if your horse has become used to climbing onto a block or "podium" as part of training (see how in my book, *The Horse Agility Handbook*), make sure he realizes that a mounting block is for you to climb on, *not* him!

2 Lead your horse *near* to the mounting block—anywhere from 2 feet (60cm) to 10 feet (3m) away. You will know if you are too close because the horse will be uncomfortable and possibly swing his hindquarters away so he can face the block instead of standing by it.

3 Lead your horse up to the mounting block. Think about your steering here; do not try and turn him too sharply to position him or he will immediately be in the wrong place beside the block. Lead him in a straight line so that when you stop he is already standing in the correct position without any further maneuvering needed on your part. Ensure he is in the same position each time you ask him to halt—this position is where you are going to get on when riding (figs. A–D).

4 When the horse can be led straight to the block, stands in the correct position and halts for a count of one, reward him, and lead him away.

5 Repeat this standing beside the block for longer and longer periods until the horse realizes that it is a comfortable place to be (fig. E).

HOW DO YOU KNOW WHEN YOU'VE DONE IT?

The horse will stand quietly and relaxed next to the block.

WHAT YOU CAN DO IF IT DOESN'T HAPPEN

• Don't assume anything here. It's interesting how many horses find this exercise quite hard, so help your horse by making the mounting block a good place to be. Hang out there, relax and make sure he is comfortable. Don't always make it the place where you get on him and go to work!

• When your horse keeps moving his hind end away from the block, you need to immediately reposition him. There is no need to get angry or frustrated, just put him back in position and let him know that is where you want him to be. If this still isn't working, you have gone too fast.

• If the horse is afraid of standing at the mounting block, move away until he feels he's at a safe distance from it. Then gradually ask him to stand closer, each time waiting for him to feel comfortable before you move on.

B. *Ask him to stand still.*

C. *It is easier to lead your horse straight to the mounting block as in A than having to reposition him, as I will here.*

A. *Lead your horse to the mounting block.*

D. *Ask him to stand in the right place—if you were riding, you should be able to get on.*

E. *Make the mounting block a nice place for the horse to be and not always about work.*

OTHER THINGS YOU CAN DO WITH THIS EXERCISE
- Use your imagination to think of different items that you could mount from and teach your horse to feel secure standing next to them.
- Start to stand on the block in preparation for mounting.

30

REQUIREMENTS
Exercise 7: Teach Standing Still

It is much safer for you when your horse is calm and controlled as you lead him through any narrow space.

HELPFUL HINT

Using a longer rope than usual may be helpful here as you must ensure you don't pull on the horse when you pass through the gap, causing him to move before you've asked him to join you.

Lead Through a Narrow Gap

WHY DO THIS?
This will help your horse be more comfortable loading into a trailer and make leading through narrow gates, doors, and into stalls and stables safer.

HOW TO DO IT
1 Use an existing narrow gap (or create one with two barrels)—anything that is safe.
2 Lead your horse to the gap and stop in front of it (fig. A).
3 Ask the horse to stand still (fig. B).
4 Pass through the gap yourself while the horse waits.
5 Ask the horse to join you (fig. C).

HOW DO YOU KNOW WHEN YOU'VE DONE IT?
The horse will wait calmly on one side of the gap until you ask him to come through and join you on the other side.

WHAT YOU CAN DO IF IT DOESN'T HAPPEN
• Make sure the horse knows how to stand still. You can help him in this by adding a visual cue (hand held up in a stop signal) or vocal cue (saying "Wait"). If you use these cues regularly he will soon connect them with standing still (see Exercise 7: Teach Standing Still).
• If the horse rushes through the gap then it is too narrow. Create a gap using barrels or use a wider gate to get this exercise solid before making it progressively narrower (fig. D).

OTHER THINGS YOU CAN DO WITH THIS EXERCISE
Load the horse into a trailer and move through gates more easily and safely (fig. E).

A. Ask your horse to walk to the gap.

B. Ask him to wait.

C. Ask him to join you.

D. You might need to make the gap much wider at first.

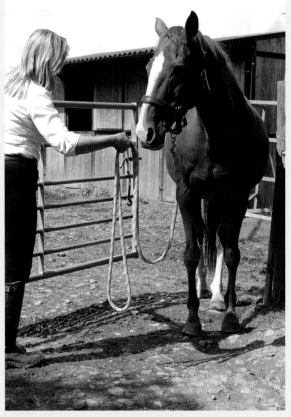

E. Leading through a narrow space is made easier this way.

GROUND EXERCISE

31

REQUIREMENTS
Exercise 7: Teach Standing Still

Teach your horse that it is safe to stand in a narrow space so he'll be more relaxed when traveling or standing in an aisle.

Stand in a Narrow Space

WHY DO THIS?
Horses are naturally claustrophobic so anything you can do to help them feel safer in a confined space will cause him to be braver in the trailer, corridors, and other tight spaces.

HOW TO DO IT
1 Create a safe, narrow gap using plastic barrels, or use an existing narrow gate or door.
2 Lead your horse to the gap.
3 Ask him to wait.
4 Pass through the gap yourself.
5 Ask the horse to walk and then halt in the gap (figs. A & B).
6 After one second, ask him to join you.
7 Repeat this, increasing the length of time the horse stands in the gap until he is happy to stay there as long as you want.

HOW DO YOU KNOW WHEN YOU'VE DONE IT?
The horse is happy to stand still in narrow gaps and confined spaces (fig. C).

WHAT YOU CAN DO IF IT DOESN'T HAPPEN
• When the horse still rushes out of the gap within one second, then one second is too long! So, instead, as he passes through the gap, just take a breath, hesitate, then ask him to move toward you. This hesitation is a thought that you want him to stop, but no more than that.
• It may be that the gap is too narrow. Make it wider to start with until he can stand in a gap maybe 10 feet (3m) wide, then progressively close the gap. If he starts to rush again, you've gone too fast.

OTHER THINGS YOU CAN DO WITH THIS EXERCISE
Ask the horse to stand still in the trailer and, in fact, any narrow space without worrying that he will feel claustrophobic.

A. Ask your horse to walk up to and part way through the gap, but give him room to move if he has to.

B. Ask him to stop and wait in the gap.

C. Try the exercise standing in the narrow gap of the trailer.

REQUIREMENTS

Exercise 6: Back Up Away from You;
27: Back Up Between Two Poles;
30: Lead through a Narrow Gap;
31: Stand in a Narrow Space

When a horse backs up
through a narrow space at
your request, it is a sign
that he trusts you.

HELPFUL HINT

As with many of these
exercises, do not rush this
one. The aim is for the horse
to be relaxed as he moves
backward.

Back Up Through a Narrow Gap

WHY DO THIS?

Being able to back your horse through a narrow gap is an exercise in trust
and requires skills in both backing up *and* steering. It is useful for loading in
and out of the trailer.

HOW TO DO IT

1 Make sure the gap you use is safe in case the horse bumps it with his
   hind end. It's best to use two plastic barrels, but a well-constructed
   doorway is suitable, too. Also check there is nothing he could back into
   on the other side of the gap that could scare or hurt him.
2 Be sure your horse is easy to back up (see Exercise 6: Back Up Away
   from You).
3 Also, he should walk calmly through the narrow space (see Exercise 30:
   Lead Through a Narrow Gap).
4 Lead him so that he is only *halfway* through the gap then ask him to
   back up.
5 Lead him *almost through* the gap then ask him to back up.
6 Lead him *right through* the gap and ask him to back through it (figs. A & B).
7 Take it one footstep at a time. If he starts to go crookedly and looks as if
   he'll bump into the barrels or sides of the door, just stop, reposition him,
   and continue backing him.

HOW DO YOU KNOW WHEN YOU'VE DONE IT?

The horse comfortably backs up through a gap without resistance or fear.

WHAT YOU CAN DO IF IT DOESN'T HAPPEN

• Do not let the horse rush this exercise. It is far better to have a horse take
  one calm measured step. A rushing horse is a scared horse.
• If the horse bumps his hind end don't make a fuss; just reposition him and
  ask for one step before finishing the session that day.

OTHER THINGS YOU CAN DO WITH THIS EXERCISE

• Back the horse through the gap without passing through it first: turn him
  around just before the gap and back him through.
• Back into a trailer (fig. C).

A. Make the gap wide to start with and lead the horse through it before you ask him to back up.

B. When you make the gap narrower, go slowly and carefully so the horse does not knock himself as he goes backward through the space.

C. When you are more practiced you can try backing into the trailer.

33

REQUIREMENTS

Exercise 6: Back Up Away from You and
Exercise 17: Move the Hind End Over

Straighten a horse
whenever he becomes
"crooked" when going
backward.

HELPFUL HINT

Slow down! Set up each step
and give the horse time to
answer the question.

Back Up While Weaving Through Markers

WHY DO THIS?

This exercise helps you with a *straight* back up. Once you know how to steer the horse's front and back end, you will know how to straighten him if he becomes crooked.

HOW TO DO IT

1. Place a line of markers along the ground in a straight line; cones are ideal. They need to be at least 12 feet (4m) apart to begin. Five of them is a good number.
2. Think of the horse's head as a steering wheel. How you move it causes his body, and therefore his feet, to move in a particular way.
3. Lead your horse forward, weaving through the cones relaxed and easily (fig. A).
4. Halt. Then ask the horse to back up through the cones trying to follow the same path as he walked when he went forward.
5. To move his hind end over: Whichever side of the horse you want to move over, push his head over to that side. So if you want to steer the horse's left hind leg over, push his head toward that leg and it will step over, thus steering the horse around the cone.
6. Now if you want to steer him in the other direction—in other words, you want his right hind leg to step over—push his head toward his right leg until he steps over (fig. B).
7. Continue asking the horse to back up and step over until he has completed the whole weave backward.

HOW DO YOU KNOW WHEN YOU'VE DONE IT?

The horse will back up in an evenly relaxed manner, weaving backward through a line of cones.

WHAT YOU CAN DO IF IT DOESN'T HAPPEN

Don't do too much to start; just one cone will do at first. Complete one step at a time and think ahead to where you want the horse to go next. When you rush, the horse will do too much, too fast, and consequently, you will over steer.

OTHER THINGS YOU CAN DO WITH THIS EXERCISE

- As you practice this exercise you will find ways of steering the front end as well. Experiment to see how many ways you can steer your horse (fig. C).
- Back around corners, circles, and in figure eights.

A. Walk the horse through the markers first.

B. Here I am steering the horse's hind end over.

C. Now I am steering the front end over.

34

REQUIREMENTS

Exercise 15: Lead with a Loose Rope;
16: Move the Front End Over;
17: Move the Hind End Over

Directing the horse's feet
from anywhere makes
you the "leader."

HELPFUL HINT

If you have trouble keeping
your feet still, try standing
on a marker or in the middle
of a hula hoop (fig. F).

Change Direction While Not Moving Your Feet

WHY DO THIS?

This helps the horse to use his hocks thus lightens his front end. It shows the horse that you can direct his feet. Allowing the horse to walk past you really means that you are the leader whatever your position in relation to the horse. Horses that walk past the human without permission are taking command, but when they trust that the handler is able to lead from anywhere, they feel secure wherever you are standing.

HOW TO DO IT

1 Walk beside your horse on a loose rein; do not get too close because he will need room to move his front end over (fig. A).
2 Stop walking; the horse will halt as well.
3 Ask him to move his hind end away and face you (figs. B & C).
4 Ask him to move his forehand over in the direction you have just walked from (fig. D).
5 You will now be on the other side of the horse without having moved your feet.
6 Now walk off in the direction you have just come from (fig. E).

HOW DO YOU KNOW WHEN YOU'VE DONE IT?

The horse will turn smoothly in one long movement by stepping under his belly with his hind leg. He will then put weight into his hocks as he steps over with his front end to face in the opposite direction.

WHAT YOU CAN DO IF IT DOESN'T HAPPEN

This exercise must be done in *slow motion* first. It looks very impressive when done at speed (fig. G), but it will frighten and confuse the horse if the foundation is not solid. Make sure each of the skills—*walking, stepping the hind end over* and *asking the front end to step over*—are solidly in place before putting it all together.

OTHER THINGS YOU CAN DO WITH THIS EXERCISE

• Instead of halting the horse, keep the forward motion and ask the horse to turn while he's moving.
• While the horse is traveling around on a longe line, turn him to go in the opposite direction in one smooth movement without him stopping before he turns.

A. Walk the horse forward on a loose rope.

B. Stop walking and ask the hind end to go away . . .

C. . . . until the horse faces you.

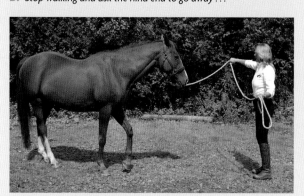

D. Ask the horse to turn his head and shoulders away.

E. Walk off in the opposite direction.

F. When you move your feet too much, stand inside a hula hoop!

G. As you get better at this you can increase the speed.

35

REQUIREMENTS

Exercise 14: Throw a Rope
Over a Horse's Head

The horse should see you
in the same way—out
of both of his eyes.

HELPFUL HINT

If you know your horse will
kick then he is not ready
for this exercise. You must
do more exercises with the
rope before you proceed.

Turn Using a Rope Over the Hocks

WHY DO THIS?

Horses do not see the world in the same way as we do. Because their eyes are on the side of their head, each eye sees the world in a different way. Some call one side the *thinking* side, the other the *flight* side. Whatever it's called, you will find that each side of your horse behaves differently. This exercise is to help your horse accept that although you suddenly appear in the "other" eye as he turns, nothing has changed. Particularly when you are going to ride, this is important because the horse will need to be aware of you from both of his eyes.

HOW TO DO IT

1. You need a long rope or longe line for this exercise, at least 12 feet (4m) long.
2. Stand beside your horse. Holding onto one end, throw the lead rope over his head so that it is on the other side of his neck. Keep the end in your hand.
3. Work the rope along his body until it is running along the other side of his body resting on his hocks (fig. A).
4. Very gently draw backward by putting the *slightest* feel onto the rope asking the horse to bend his head away (fig. B). You want him to follow the feel of the rope and turn right around to face you. Don't pull! Set it up and wait (fig. C).
5. When the horse faces you reward him (fig. D).

HOW DO YOU KNOW WHEN YOU'VE DONE IT?

The horse will turn away from you and almost pirouette around to face you.

WHAT YOU CAN DO IF IT DOESN'T HAPPEN

• If the horse becomes concerned by the rope around his body you need to do a lot more work with a rope as outlined in Exercise 14 (p. 36).
• When you put slight pressure on the rope to ask the horse to turn, just wait. Give him time to work out the answer. When he gives even a tiny bit, release the tension slightly to let him know he's on the right track. As he starts to turn, do not pull him; just keep the rope out of the way so that he doesn't tread on it.
• If you are concerned that your horse may kick, use a longer rope and hold onto his head while you feed the rope over his back and onto his hocks. When you start to ask him to turn, step back to being level with his head. This will ensure that you are as far as possible away from the hind end (fig. E).

OTHER THINGS YOU CAN DO WITH THIS EXERCISE

This exercise stands alone.

A. Put the rope over the other side of the horse so it is resting on his hocks.

B. Draw back, asking the head to move away from you, and put only a very little bit of tension in the rope.

C. Allow him to turn.

D. Reward him as he comes around to face you.

E. You can use a longer rope when you don't feel safe near the horse's hind end.

PART TWO

IN THE SADDLE

Exercises 36–60

GROUND SKILLS TO RIDING SKILLS—MAKING LIFE SIMPLE!

When you've worked through all, or some, of the *3-Minute Ground Exercises* you'll be well on your way to having created a safer riding horse. All the concepts and ideas in Part One can be related to ridden work because you have physically learned how to achieve the same maneuver on the ground so you can use and adapt it to being on the horse's back, or because you now understand the concepts behind what you are trying to achieve.

Some riding problems are just too challenging for most of us to solve while in the saddle but quite a few of these can be sorted out on the ground. But this doesn't mean you work the horse so hard that he's exhausted or too scared to do anything more than plod around when you get on. It's about moving him around on the ground in a deliberate constructive fashion that leads him to understand your request and believe that he can, at least, have a try at answering the question.

A classic ground-skill-to-ridden exercise is Move Sideways (Exercise 41). If you start by moving the horse sideways on the ground—front end; back end; then both together (Exercise 18)—when you actually get on and ride, you will see that you do a very similar thing. The simplicity is that you know the horse can already do it— and so does the horse!

What you can do on the horse's back: I am touching my horse on her side with my leg in exactly the same place as I did when I was on the ground (see photo on p. 9). My near-side rein quietly discourages any forward or backward steps. On her off side, the rein and my leg are soft, giving her space to move into.

36

REQUIREMENTS

Exercise 1: Being Still Around a Horse and Exercise 7: Teach Standing Still

Standing still is one of the most important things a horse must learn to do.

HELPFUL HINTS

• Remember that you must be still for your horse to be still.
• Don't look for too much to start with. He may only give you a slight feeling of standing still at the beginning so look out for that moment and acknowledge it when it happens.

Teach a Horse to Stand Still

WHY DO THIS?

For safety, the rider always needs to be ready before the horse moves so the horse must learn to wait until he is *asked* to move off.

HOW TO DO IT

1. As soon as you get onto your horse, be still. Do not immediately pick up the reins as if you expect the horse to move off, though you will be holding them, of course. Sit still and make sure you are relaxed in your whole body. Breathe and be quiet; the horse should stand absolutely still until you ask him to move (figs. A–C).
2. If he moves as you sit there, bring him back to the same place either by turning him or backing him up. To start with only ask him to stand for the count of one. As he begins to understand that he must stand still, you can ask for a bit longer every day.

HOW DO YOU KNOW WHEN YOU'VE DONE IT?

As you mount and settle into the saddle, the horse does not move or shift his feet; he is completely still.

WHAT YOU CAN DO IF IT DOESN'T HAPPEN

Some horses think they must move off as soon as the rider is on board. When you feel this happening, stop your horse's movement and ask him to stand. Reward him as soon as you feel him stop, or even hesitate, before riding on. Do not fight him to keep still; look for understanding that you are asking him not to move and reward that. These moments of understanding will get longer.

Note: You cannot expect your horse to stand still if *you* are distracted or fidgeting or moving about! *You* must be still, too (fig. D).

OTHER THINGS YOU CAN DO WITH THIS EXERCISE

• Asking a horse to stand still is useful in all aspects of riding, from the required discipline of a dressage test to standing at a junction in the road waiting for a safe moment to move out.
• At any time you are out on the trail, just ask your horse to stop for a while so that you can breathe and look at the view.

A. Sit still on your horse.

B. Reward the horse quietly. I am gently touching my horse's withers to thank her for being still.

C. Your horse should stand still anywhere and wait for your request to move off.

D. You cannot expect your horse to stand still if you are not giving him your attention.

37

REQUIREMENTS

Exercise 12: Bend the Head Around to the Side and 13: Bend the Head Away to the Opposite Side—these help you to feel the flexing movement and establish whether the horse is physically and emotionally able to complete the exercise.

Bending (flexing) the horse's head around toward your leg demonstrates his ability to be supple.

HELPFUL HINT

• Make sure you are feeling relaxed in your seat. When your legs and buttocks are tight, the horse will find this exercise much harder because you will be blocking his rib movement.
• Don't allow the horse to snatch his head back to the front. When he is softly bent you can allow him to return his head forward again either by leaning forward and gently pushing his nose away, or brushing the ribs on the opposite side to straighten him.

Flex the Head Around to the Side

WHY DO THIS?

It demonstrates that that your horse is supple and ready to work. Eventually this move forms part of the Emergency Stop Rein, an important skill that one day could save your life!

HOW TO DO IT

1 Sit still on your horse.
2 Make sure you are relaxed and not stiff anywhere in your body.
3 Hold the reins in your left hand. You are going to ask the horse to bring his nose around to the right.
4 Reach down the right rein with your right hand, but do not tip your body over. Simply ask him to bring his nose around toward your right foot, your knee, or somewhere in between (figs. A–C).
5 Hold the rein, do not try and pull the horse around. Wait.
6 Wait and feel for the slightest give. This *never* takes longer than three minutes!
7 With each "give" to your "ask," release the rein slightly before asking again.
8 To bend the horse's head around to the other side, simply reverse these instructions.

HOW DO YOU KNOW WHEN YOU'VE DONE IT?

When the horse is relaxed about turning his nose around to you with the slightest ask.

WHAT YOU CAN DO IF IT DOESN'T HAPPEN

• While you are asking the horse to bend, brush his side with your leg near the girth on the same side. This helps to free the ribs, which will move away, causing the horse to tip his nose around.
• Look for that moment of give from the horse and release as you feel it happen.
• If the horse moves his feet, you are doing too much; relax and ask again.

OTHER THINGS YOU CAN DO WITH THIS EXERCISE

This exercise can be expanded into a turn on the forehand. See if you can ask for the bend without using the rein. Brush the side of the horse with your leg. Watch the ear on the same side. When that ear flicks back it is the start of the bend. Reward and ask again. Eventually, you will be able to do this exercise without the reins at all.

A. Pick up the rein and ask the horse to bring his head around.

B. The horse is resisting here, so I just sit and wait.

C. Using the rein for this exercise is only a suggestion: If your body language is right your horse will flex without it.

RIDDEN EXERCISE

38

REQUIREMENTS

**Exercise 8: Back Up a
Horse While Beside Him**

Backing up requires hock
engagement, which
promotes desired
impulsion.

HELPFUL HINT

Look for one free-moving
step only. Once the horse
can do one step, you can
just ask him to keep
repeating it!

Backing Up

WHY DO THIS?

Being able to back up your horse has many practical applications, but it also prepares your horse for other movements by engaging his hocks: Because his hind legs are farther underneath his body, he has more impulsion.

HOW TO DO IT

First, let's consider a don't: *Don't* pull back on both reins!

1 Prepare your horse for the movement; sit up.
2 Put a little tension on the reins to "close the front door."
3 Raise your energy level as if you are going to ride forward.
4 Focus on a point in front of you at head height and ride *back* from it.
5 When you get one step, stop asking and reward (figs. A–E).

HOW DO YOU KNOW WHEN YOU'VE DONE IT?

The horse will rock back, then take a step back.

WHAT YOU CAN DO IF IT DOESN'T HAPPEN

• Decide which front foot is farther forward than the other. This is the foot that is going to step back next. Raise the rein on that side and vibrate it while you wait for the horse to show some understanding. This frees up the shoulder thus helping the foot become free. As soon as that foot moves back, stop asking.
• Make sure you are not leaning forward or looking down, as these positions will put weight on the horse's front foot, which then becomes more difficult for him to pick up.
• There should be no resistance in the backing up. You will know he is resisting when his head comes up or gets tucked right into his chest.

OTHER THINGS YOU CAN DO WITH THIS EXERCISE

At first, you will look for any backward steps, but eventually, you want the horse to go back in "two time." This means that the diagonal pairs of legs move at the same time, which is a *true* back up.

A. *Sit still on the horse before you ask him to move.*

B. *"Ride backward" on your horse; do not pull him back.*

C. *When you pull, you lock up the horse's hind end so he overbends.*

D. *Backing up is two-time movement. Here is one diagonal pair of legs stepping backward . . .*

E. *. . . and the other diagonal pair of legs stepping backward.*

39

Move the Front End Over

REQUIREMENTS

Exercise 16: Move the Front End Over. This exercise helps you understand what you are looking for when in the saddle.

When you can move the front end over you know that the horse is using his hocks.

WHY DO THIS?
It helps to lighten the horse's front end thus engaging his hocks. It is also useful when opening and closing a gate from the saddle.

HOW TO DO IT
1 Sit up on your horse.
2 Hold the reins in both hands.
3 To turn the front end over to the right:
   • The left rein stops the horse going forward.
   • The right rein comes away from the neck, creating a space for the horse to move his shoulders into.
   • The left leg stays softly against the girth.
   • The right leg comes slightly away from the girth (figs. A & B).
4 Look where you want to go—that is, not down but *up to the right*. You are "closing the door" to forward and "opening a door" to create a space for the shoulders to move into.
5 The horse may move his right or left front leg first. Don't worry to start; just let him move his shoulders over.

HOW DO YOU KNOW WHEN YOU'VE DONE IT?
The shoulders of the horse will travel around to the right.

WHAT YOU CAN DO IF IT DOESN'T HAPPEN
• Just wait: Set it up as described above and wait for a minute. When nothing happens, vibrate the right rein up and out, and look up and out. If there is still no response, bring your left foot forward and tap the horse's shoulder. Wait. The horse will do something that indicates he is *thinking* in that direction. Reward the thought by relaxing slightly or telling him "Good boy!"
• If the horse tries to walk forward, use your left rein to stop him.
• Sometimes, if you first ask the horse to take a step back, it puts his weight back on the hocks, which releases the front feet. This makes it easier for the horse to move them over.
• You may have to exaggerate your movements so the horse understands you are asking him to do something specific (fig. C).

OTHER THINGS YOU CAN DO WITH THIS EXERCISE
• Describe a complete turn through 360 degrees, turning on the hindquarters.
• It teaches a horse to use his hocks instead of "pulling" himself forward with his front legs.

> **HELPFUL HINT**
>
> **Don't pull. This sets up a tug of war that is impossible for you to win. Set the exercise up and wait.**

A. *Use an opening rein on the side you want your horse to move over to.*

B. *Close your left rein and left leg (the opposite side) so the horse wants to move into the open space made by the right rein and right leg.*

C. *You may have to exaggerate to teach!*

Move the Hind End Over

REQUIREMENTS

Exercise 12: Bend the Head Around to the Side; 13: Bend the Head Away to the Opposite Side; 17: Move the Hind End Over. These exercises on the ground tell you what happens to the horse's body. With a very stiff horse it is easier, and often safer, to start on the ground because if he resists a horse may become quite "active" while expressing his feelings!

Disengaging the hindquarters gives the rider control of the horse's speed and direction.

HELPFUL HINT

Don't try and force this. The horse should feel supple, relaxed and free as he bends, then steps over.

WHY DO THIS?

Being able to move your horse's hindquarters over shows that he is loose and supple in his hips. Done correctly, it shows that the horse has released his whole body to the handler. It is often called: "Disengaging the hindquarters." Being able to control the hind end means the rider is in control of the speed and direction of the horse. It is also useful for opening and closing a gate and helps with canter lead changes.

HOW TO DO IT

1 Sit still on your horse.
2 Reach down the right rein without leaning over and ask the horse to bring his nose around to your knee. It should feel relaxed and free. The horse must keep his nose around throughout this exercise. If at any time you lose this bend you must get it back before continuing. Remember if your horse is trying to stay straight, he's thinking of leaving without your permission so make sure you keep him bent!
3 Remember to release the left rein on the other side or the horse will not be able to move his head around.
4 Put your right leg on the horse's side.
5 Make sure your left leg is not pushing on the opposite side; the horse needs space to step into on the left side.
6 The horse should step his right hind leg underneath his body from right to left; the front end should stay still or walk on the spot (figs. A–C).
7 As soon as he steps over, stop asking with your leg, release the rein, and reward.

HOW DO YOU KNOW WHEN YOU'VE DONE IT?

You will feel the hindquarters move over to the left.

WHAT YOU CAN DO IF IT DOESN'T HAPPEN

• If the horse just doesn't move, wait. If he still hasn't moved after two-and-a-half minutes, take the reins in your left hand, reach back with your right hand and tap his right hip (fig. D). Make sure you keep your right leg on his side and the left leg off his other side to give him room to move. Do not try and "push" him over because he will just push back. Keep tapping his hip with more and more energy until you feel the slightest movement to the left. Stop and reward. The next time you ask it should be easier.
• What if you get more than one step? You are doing too much. Do less and remember to stop asking him to move as soon as he seems to be about to take a step.

OTHER THINGS YOU CAN DO WITH THIS EXERCISE.

• As a ridden exercise it can save your life as an Emergency Stop Rein. You can start to repeat this at walk and trot. When you exaggerate this movement it becomes a useful method of stopping quickly.
• As you develop your horsemanship you will find that there are many patterns that incorporate this movement.

A. Ask for the flex, then lift your energy level, touch his side with your leg and the horse will step underneath his belly.

B. This is what it looks like from behind.

C. As you practice this you can become very subtle in your cues.

D. If the horse gets stuck, don't kick; just keep asking and lean back to tap him on the hip. This will encourage the horse to step over.

41

REQUIREMENTS

Exercises 39 & 40: Moving the Front and Hind End Over, both need to be solid before you start on this sideways exercise.

Being able to move your horse sideways will help with lateral work.

Ensure you can move the front and hind ends over smoothly without resistance before you start on sideways. Going sideways on a horse is such an impressive-looking movement, we often rush through the preparation to get there. Stiffness can then ruin the movement.

Move Sideways

WHY DO THIS?

This is a great way to loosen up your horse and help him feel more elastic. It's also very useful when maneuvering the horse around gates and corrals.

HOW TO DO IT

It is really just moving the horse's front end over, then *immediately* moving the hind end over. But don't rush it. Give the horse the chance to answer each individual request for a movement before going onto the next.

1 Ask the horse to move his shoulders over one step to the right (Exercise 39, p. 88). This means you close your left leg and left rein; and open your right rein and right leg (fig. A).

2 Ask the horse to move his hindquarters over one step to the right (Exercise 40, p. 90). This means you ask the horse to flex to the left; put your left leg on; and ask his left hind leg to step underneath him (fig. B).

3 Repeat Steps 1 and 2 smoothly one after the other until there is a seamless continuity in the movement (fig. C).

4 As the horse learns the pattern, the feeling of moving the front end over and then moving the back end over will diminish, and the horse will just *move sideways*.

HOW DO YOU KNOW WHEN YOU'VE DONE IT?

The horse will step sideways with no forward or backward movement.

WHAT YOU CAN DO IF IT DOESN'T HAPPEN

• Always check that you are not blocking his movement with your weight, your legs, or your reins, and that you have created a space for the horse to move into.

• Make sure the horse is consistently moving his front end and hind end separately whenever you ask for it.

• If he keeps moving forward when you ask, do this exercise with a fence in front of you to prevent this from happening. If he keeps moving backward, try using a pole on the ground behind you.

OTHER THINGS YOU CAN DO WITH THIS EXERCISE

Try side-passing over a pole or an object such as a cone or bucket. Start this by riding over a pole until his front feet are on one side and hind feet on the other. Stop, then ask the horse to go sideways: The pole should remain between his front and back legs under his belly as he moves. When he can do this, ride him into position at the end of the pole and side-pass along the complete length of the pole. You can then sidepass over other safe objects.

A. *Here, I am asking the front end to move over.*

B. *Now, I am asking the hind end to move over.*

C. *Everything is moving together.*

42

REQUIREMENTS
None

Focus your riding on
what *you* want the
horse to do. Stop
being a passenger.

Focus Your Riding

WHY DO THIS?
We frequently allow the horse to choose his own speed and direction, so when we ask him to do what we want, we are surprised that he won't! This exercise is about you no longer being a passenger and taking control of the horse's feet!

HOW TO DO IT
1. This can be done in an arena or out on a trail ride or hack.
2. Look ahead and choose a point to ride to (figs. A & B). As soon as you reach that point, either change direction or change your speed. When you get better at it, you will be able to do both at the same time.
3. Be very precise: Do not let the horse drift from the point you have chosen to focus on by changing his speed or direction.

HOW DO YOU KNOW WHEN YOU'VE DONE IT?
Your horse will change his speed and/or his direction *only* at the exact spot you selected.

WHAT YOU CAN DO IF IT DOESN'T HAPPEN
Slow down and perhaps halt at each spot before changing direction or speed. This will give the horse time to understand that *you* are taking control of his feet.

OTHER THINGS YOU CAN DO WITH THIS EXERCISE
This will help you ride accurately by training you to focus on *where* and *how* you want to reach a destination.

A. *Look where you want to go and go there . . .*

B. *. . . even when your horse might be having other ideas!*

REQUIREMENTS

Exercise 30: Lead Through
a Narrow Gap

To safely ride through a
narrow gap you need to
focus and steer your
horse accurately.

HELPFUL HINT

When out for a ride the
gates or gaps you need to
pass through often cannot
be adjusted. When there is
room for the horse with his
saddle but not your legs as
well, you should dismount
and lead him through or put
your legs over his shoulders
(fig. D). Please ensure
that your horse is used to
this rather unusual riding
position before you try this
out on the trail!

Ride Through a Narrow Gap

WHY DO THIS?
If you've ever caught your knee on a gatepost as you ride through a gate, you'll know why you want to be in control in these sort of situations!

HOW TO DO IT
1 When practicing this exercise, for safety, you can adjust the width of your gap made with cones, barrels, or other obstacles.
2 Ride to the gap and, before you go through, stop.
3 Assess if the gap is wide enough for the horse carrying you and your saddle to fit through.
4 Ask the horse to pass through the gap one step at a time, pausing as necessary. This should be done calmly without any change in speed (figs. A–C).

HOW DO YOU KNOW WHEN YOU'VE DONE IT?
You will reach the other side without catching your knees or saddle on the sides of the gap.

WHAT YOU CAN DO IF IT DOESN'T HAPPEN
• If your knees or saddle touch the sides of the obstacle, either the gap is too narrow for you to pass through or you have not steered right through the middle.
• Go right back to slowing the horse down. Work with him on the ground to find out exactly what the problem is. Asking him to stand in the gap while wearing his saddle will build his confidence if he's anxious.
• Once a horse has caught the saddle in a narrow gap, he often loses his confidence, so you may need to go back to where he feels braver and build the skill from the bottom up.

OTHER THINGS YOU CAN DO WITH THIS EXERCISE
Back your horse through the gap.

A. *Look ahead through the gap and ride through confidently.*

B. *If your horse rushes, walk through one step at a time.*

C. *Make "friends" of the barrels—make them a nice place for the horse to be.*

D. *When a gap is very narrow you can lift your legs up onto the horse's shoulders—see the helpful hint on p. 96.*

RIDDEN EXERCISE

44

REQUIREMENTS

Exercise 25: Walk Over
Unusual Surfaces

Getting the horse used to
all types of footing is a
confidence and trust-
building exercise.

HELPFUL HINT

Make sure you practice
this exercise on the ground
first. A horse shying
and leaping away from
something like a tarpaulin
on the ground can unseat
the rider in the process.

Ride Over Unusual Surfaces

WHY DO THIS?
Teach your horse to be braver and safer out on the trail by being able to cope with the different surfaces.

HOW TO DO IT
1 Start with a tarpaulin, flat board, or other non-slip material.
2 Ride your horse toward the new surface (fig. A).
3 As soon as you feel him hesitate (if he does), stop.
4 Relax.
5 Wait for your horse to relax.
6 Ride him away from the surface and repeat Steps 2 through 5 until he walks over the surface (figs. B–D).

HOW DO YOU KNOW WHEN YOU'VE DONE IT?
The horse will confidently cross the new surface without hesitation.

WHAT YOU CAN DO IF IT DOESN'T HAPPEN
You have gone too fast. In the first session you may only achieve the horse calmly *looking* at the surface. This can be enough for him for that day. The horse should never feel so frightened that he needs to leap about or want to run away.

OTHER THINGS YOU CAN DO WITH THIS EXERCISE
This technique works for going past strange objects and crossing through water—to name a couple of advantages (fig. E).

A. *Allow the horse look at the new surface.*

B. *Never be afraid to reward the horse by riding away.*

C. *Let the horse explore what it feels like.*

D. *Ask him to stand on the new surface when he feels confident.*

E. *A horse that is allowed to explore new things is more open to them when you are out for a ride.*

REQUIREMENTS

Exercise 26: Back Up Over a Pole
and 38: Backing Up

Your horse shows
that he is trusting
and supple when you
can ride him backward
over a pole without his
feet touching it.

HELPFUL HINT

Take the time that you need
to get this exercise right.
Three minutes is plenty of
time to get a *thought* of
going backward into the
horse's head. And, stop
immediately when you get
even a suggestion of backing
up—this will cause the horse
to become braver. If you try
to force a frightened horse,
you only increase his fear.

Back Up Over a Pole

WHY DO THIS?

This is a trust exercise but it can also be very useful in a real-life riding situation: for example, should you need to get your horse out of a tight spot in the woods and there's no way to turn around. It really helps you be more accurate when backing up and helps the horse learn to lift his feet, rather than shuffling back.

HOW TO DO IT

1 Use a half-pole or one that will not roll or move if the horse drags his feet over it when backing up.
2 Ride your horse across the pole until his front feet are just over it (fig. A).
3 Stop and wait.
4 Initially, he may want to look down and check where the pole is. Allow him to do this.
5 Ask the horse to back up over the pole (fig. B).
7 Repeat the exercise, eventually beginning with all four feet across the pole before backing up.

HOW DO YOU KNOW WHEN YOU'VE DONE IT?

The horse backs up willingly over the pole without touching it.

WHAT YOU CAN DO IF IT DOESN'T HAPPEN

• When the horse knocks the pole—an indication that he is not lifting his feet—it is a sign of resistance. Ensure that you are not blocking him by looking down (remember, eyeballs are heavy!) or by being stiff in your hips. Do not try to pull him backward—think (and only think) about lifting each foot up and over the pole. You may have to exaggerate to teach this by gently lifting each rein in time with his feet (fig. C).
• When the horse really cannot back over the pole but twists and turns to avoid doing so, you will need to put a lot more time into making the pole a nice place to be. Remember, the main reason horses find this difficult is because they are afraid. Getting angry and tough won't make them braver.

OTHER THINGS YOU CAN DO WITH THIS EXERCISE

• You can raise the pole slightly.
• Back up over a log that is larger in circumference than the pole.

A. Let the horse stand across the pole.

B. First, just back up the front feet over the pole.

C. If the horse drags his feet, lift the rein on the side of his "sticky" foot to encourage him to lift it up.

46

REQUIREMENTS
Exercise 38: Backing Up

Riding in a straight line is one of the most difficult things to be good at; use poles to help guide you.

HELPFUL HINT

The firmer you are in asking for the backup, the more likely the horse will be resistant. Set the question up, and just wait. Stop and reward while your horse is straight—never when he is crooked. This is the essence of *3-Minute Horsemanship*.

Back Up Between Two Poles

WHY DO THIS?
This exercise will help you to ride with more straightness, both forward and backward. It also accustoms your horse to passing through narrow spaces.

HOW TO DO IT?
1 The aim of this exercise is to back up the horse in a straight line without touching the poles. The poles can be short or long; set wide apart or very narrow. Start where you and your horse are most comfortable.
2 Ride the horse through the poles until just his front feet are beyond the end of the poles (fig. A).
4 Ask him to back up. Be slow and deliberate asking for one step at a time (fig. B).
5 If he goes crookedly you will have to reposition him (fig. C and see below).
6 Keep asking until all four feet are beyond the pole corridor.
7 Now ride the horse right through the corridor until all four feet are beyond it, then back up through it as before.

HOW DO YOU KNOW WHEN YOU'VE DONE IT?
The horse will have backed through the pole corridor without touching the poles on either side.

WHAT YOU CAN DO IF IT DOESN'T HAPPEN
• Start with a shorter corridor or with a larger width between the poles and build up to a longer, narrower corridor. Look for one straight, willing step and stop there.
• If the horse starts to go crookedly, you can straighten him: As his hind end starts to move over, turn his head toward that side. Sometimes brushing the area behind the girth with your leg helps the horse here, and he will step over to become straight again. Start backing the horse when he is just a few steps into the pole corridor, and build up to going farther and farther through.
• Crookedness is a resistance; don't fight it, just gently correct.

OTHER THINGS YOU CAN DO WITH THIS EXERCISE
Back through gateways and narrow gaps.

A. *First, start by walking through the poles until only the horse's front feet are beyond the end of the corridor.*

B. *Do not pull the horse back; ask him to step back calmly through the poles.*

C. *When your horse goes crookedly like this, correct him by putting your left leg just behind the girth to ask his left hind leg to step back into the pole corridor.*

RIDDEN EXERCISE

47

REQUIREMENTS

Exercise 36: Teach a Horse to Stand Still

When your horse can stand quietly in a narrow space, he will not feel he has to rush through because of feeling trapped.

Stand in a Narrow Space

WHY DO THIS?

Horses are naturally claustrophobic so anything you can do to help them feel safer in confined places will cause them to be braver in corridors, stalls, and tight spaces.

HOW TO DO IT

1 Create a narrow gap using plastic barrels. Or use a safe gateway or doorway.
2 Ride your horse through the gap (fig. A).
3 Next, ride into the gap and ask for a pause; count *one* second and ride out (fig. B).
4 Repeat until the horse is offering the halt; then count *two* seconds before riding out.
5 Repeat and increase the length of time the horse stands in the gap until he is happy to stay there as long as you ask him to (fig. C).

HOW DO YOU KNOW WHEN YOU'VE DONE IT?

The horse is happy to stand still in a relaxed way in narrow gaps and confined spaces.

WHAT YOU CAN DO IF IT DOESN'T HAPPEN

• If the horse still rushes out when you have only counted to one, then one is too long! As he passes through the gap, instead take a breath and hesitate, then ask him to move on. The hesitation is a thought that you want him to stop, but no more than that. Do not be tempted to pull on the reins to try and force him to stand in the gap. It should feel easy for the horse to do.
• It may be that the gap is too narrow; make it wider to start, maybe 10 feet (3m), then progressively close it. If the horse starts to rush again, you've gone too fast.

OTHER THINGS YOU CAN DO WITH THIS EXERCISE

It makes opening and closing a gate while on the trail much more controlled and safer.

A. *Ride through the narrow gap first.*

B. *As you pass through, pause, then ask the horse to move on. Here, I am touching the barrel as we come to a stop.*

C. *Ask him to stand for longer periods in the narrow gap.*

48

REQUIREMENTS

Exercise 14: Throw a Rope over a Horse's Head and practice throwing a rope without your horse first, so if you make a mistake, no harm is done.

A useful desensitizing exercise.

HELPFUL HINTS

• Practice rope skills, both left- and right-handed away from the horse first. Do not move on too quickly: trust lost, while swinging a rope over a horse's head, will take a long time to regain.

• Never throw the very end of the rope near the horse's head because it could flick into his eye, causing injury.

Throw a Rope Over a Horse's Head

WHY DO THIS?

Whether you are going to start lassoing from the back of your horse or not, getting him used to a rope swinging around his head will build trust. He is less likely to panic should your reins suddenly end up over his ears or face because he has already learned that ropes are not dangerous.

HOW TO DO IT

1 You will need the horse wearing a halter with a very long lead rope—between 10 feet and 12 feet (3 to 3.5 meters) is a good length. For extra safety, you may want to put a bridle on the horse as well so you can hold onto the reins for more control.

2 Make sure that when you hold your rope it is long enough so it can be swung clear of the horse's ears (fig. A).

3 Do not lean forward over the horse's neck toward his head when you start this. Sit back so that your face is well out of the way because he may throw his head in surprise when you begin.

4 Initially, drape the rope over his neck and ears just as you did on the ground (fig. B).

5 Build up to throwing the rope like a skipping rope over his head well clear of his ears. You are gently throwing the rope, being careful that it does not hurt the horse by slapping on him.

6 Increase the arc of the swing until the rope swings right over the horse's head, keeping clear of his ears (fig. C).

HOW DO YOU KNOW WHEN YOU'VE DONE IT?

The horse stands still and accepts the rope swinging over his head from one side of his neck to the other.

WHAT YOU CAN DO IF IT DOESN'T HAPPEN

Either you've moved on too fast for the horse to accept each stage, or your rope skills need further practice away from the horse.

OTHER THINGS YOU CAN DO WITH THIS EXERCISE

This skill will help prepare your horse to accept a rider roping from the saddle. When riding with one rein it enables you to throw the rein over to the other side of the horse's head without having to pass it under his neck—a move that could unbalance you and the horse, especially when going at a faster pace.

A. *Use a long rope to ensure you get good clearance over the horse's head as you throw it.*

B. *Drape the rope over the head and neck to check that he is comfortable with it.*

C. *Make sure you let the rope out long enough to go clear over the horse's ears when you begin to swing it.*

RIDDEN EXERCISE

49

REQUIREMENTS
None

Become more particular
and accurate in your
ridden work.

HELPFUL HINT

Rhythm in the movement
will really help here. Count
your steps out loud if you
have to, like the ticking of a
clock. Or, ride to music!

Walk Forward and Backward a Specific Number of Steps

WHY DO THIS?

This exercise helps you to be more consistently accurate with movements. We are all lazy when we ride, allowing the horse to drift into a halt without considering what this might be teaching him. Counting steps between starting and stopping helps you to begin to become more particular about the quality of your ridden work.

HOW TO DO IT

1 From halt, ride your horse forward five steps and stop. This isn't six steps, four steps, or even five-and-a-bit! It is *five* steps with the front feet—the front feet are easy to see so that's a good starting point. But if you do want to count five steps of the hind feet, that's just as good.

2 Right front, left front, right front, left front, right front, STOP!

3 Now ask the horse to back up five steps: right front, left front, right front, left front, right front, STOP!

4 When this is working, choose to walk a different number of steps forward then a different number of steps back. It doesn't matter how many forward or backward steps you do as long as the horse takes the number of steps you planned in advance.

HOW DO YOU KNOW WHEN YOU'VE DONE IT?

The horse walks forward in time with your count, stops, and walks backward in time with your count, then stops. You will feel in synchrony with your horse.

WHAT YOU CAN DO IF IT DOESN'T HAPPEN

The biggest mistake is when you don't prepare the horse for the stop. If you are planning to take five steps forward, you need to start planning the stop on step number *two*. As with any exercise, you must prepare a horse for the maneuver.

OTHER THINGS YOU CAN DO WITH THIS EXERCISE

Choose a specific point or mark to ride to and stop there. Become aware of how your horse will start to feel your subtle body-language cues that are telling him you're going to ask him to walk, stop, and back up (figs. A–C).

A. *Choose a marker to help you be particular about where you stop.*

B. *If the horse goes past the marker, correct him.*

C. *Back up or turn the horse to stop where you wanted to.*

RIDDEN EXERCISE

50

REQUIREMENTS

Exercise 23: Place the Front Feet and 39: Move the Front End Over. I highly recommend you review the ground exercise because it helps you to understand what is happening in the riding exercise.

When you can choose which foot to move you can be very accurate in how you maneuver your horse.

HELPFUL HINTS

• Be patient.
• Be prepared to experiment with the rein to see how it can be used to communicate with the front feet.

Place the Front Feet

WHY DO THIS?

If you can pick up and place your horse's foot anywhere, you can do anything. Riding is all about causing the horse's feet to become your own.

HOW TO DO IT

1   Sit quietly on your horse. If he is standing square it will be easier, but it's not essential.
2   Hold the reins as you normally would with your thumbs on top.
3   You are going to move the left front foot of the horse (fig. A).
4   Raise your energy as if you are going to give the instruction to walk forward; lift the left rein up and forward. You are not making the rein looser or tighter, you are just changing the feel for the horse.
5   As soon as he starts to bring that foot forward, stop asking, and he will place it on the ground and leave it there. If he steps again, you did not stop asking soon enough.
6   Now you are going to ask him to put the foot back where it was. Rock your weight back and drop your left hand back toward you. This will cause the horse to pick the left foot up and put it back where he started.
7   Now you are going to ask the horse to put that foot out to the side, stepping out to the left. Lift your left hand up, opening your shoulder and rolling your knuckles upward. You lift your hand up and out to the side and the horse will step up and out to the side.
8   To ask him to put that foot back, repeat the exercise on the right side of the horse. This will cause him to want to step with his right leg. Because he has just stepped out to the side with his left foot he will want to move that one back first to balance himself, thus returning it to the original position. Stop as soon as you feel him move or he will move the right leg as well.
9   You are now able to ask one front foot to go forward, backward, left, and right.
10   For the right foot just reverse the left and right instructions above.

HOW DO YOU KNOW WHEN YOU'VE DONE IT?

You will be able sit on your horse and move his front feet wherever you wish.

WHAT YOU CAN DO IF IT DOESN'T HAPPEN

• Be careful you are not looking down to see if the foot has moved. This puts weight onto the foot you want him to move, which he will then find difficult to pick up.
• You may have to exaggerate to teach! Don't worry. You are not going to ride around looking like a frantic windmill forever. As the horse understands what you need him to do, you can do less and less when you ask him.

OTHER THINGS YOU CAN DO WITH THIS EXERCISE

Once you can ask the horse to pick up both front feet you can easily get your horse to stand squarely.

A. *In this photo, I am "speaking" to the horse's near side front foot.*

RIDDEN EXERCISE

51

REQUIREMENTS

Exercise 24: Place the Hind Feet and
Exercise 40: Move the Hind End Over

Control the horse's
"engine" through
his hind feet.

HELPFUL HINT

Think about how you did this on the ground (Exercise 24); use the same hand movement and see your leg as extra help to shape the horse up and enable him to step under.

Place the Hind Feet

WHY DO THIS?
When you can accurately get the horse to pick up and move the hind feet, you know you are in control of his engine.

HOW TO DO IT
1 Sit quietly on your horse. If he is standing squarely it will be easier, but it's not essential.
2 Hold the reins as you normally would with your thumbs on top.
3 You are going to move the right hind foot of the horse under his belly.
4 Ask the horse to slightly bring his nose around to you on the right side.
5 Push your right elbow into your ribs and turn your fingernails upward. You are not making the rein looser or tighter, you are just changing the feel for the horse.
6 You should find that he now appears to be curved around your right leg.
7 Lift your energy level so that the horse feels he needs to be more active in his body.
8 Brush your right leg against his side just behind the girth.
9 He should start to step under his body with his right hind foot (fig. A).
10 As soon as you feel him starting to step, stop asking or you will get two steps, and you only want one to start.
11 Now you are going to ask him to put the foot back where it started. Repeat everything you did above but do it from the left side. This will cause his right foot to step back to where it was.
12 To place the left hind foot, just swap the right and left directions given above.

HOW DO YOU KNOW WHEN YOU'VE DONE IT?
You will be able to sit on your horse and cause him to step either hind foot under his body whenever you wish.

WHAT YOU CAN DO IF IT DOESN'T HAPPEN
• Some horses are very stiff and find this exercise difficult to start. You may need to lean back, put both reins in your left hand and with your right hand tap his hip to encourage him to step under with his hind foot.
• Don't get firmer if he finds this difficult. Just keep asking. It never takes longer than *three minutes* to get close to the answer you are looking for.

OTHER THINGS YOU CAN DO WITH THIS EXERCISE
Once you can move both hind feet, as and how you wish, you can ask your horse to stand square.

A. *I am asking my horse to pick up the off side hind—it needs lots of concentration from both of us! There is more tension here than I would like.*

REQUIREMENTS

Exercise 38: Backing Up;
39: Move the Front End Over; and
40: Move the Hind End Over

Perfecting your steering
while going backward.

HELPFUL HINT

Slow down! Set up each step
and give the horse time to
answer the question.

Back Up While Weaving Through Markers

WHY DO THIS?

This really helps the horse to back up straight. Once you know how to steer the horse's front and hind end, you will know how to straighten your backup when it's crooked.

HOW TO DO IT

1 Place a line of markers along the ground in a straight line—cones are ideal. They need to be at least 12 feet (4 m) apart to begin. Five cones are a good number.

2 Think of the horse's head as a steering wheel. How you move the horse's head will cause his body, and therefore his feet, to move in a particular way.

3 Ride your horse forward at walk through the cones, weaving through relaxed and easily

4 Halt beyond the last cone and ask the horse to back up, weaving through the cones. Try to have him follow the same path that he walked going forward through the cones (fig. A).

5 When you want to steer the front end, think of "lifting" the horse's head, shoulders, and consequently, his front feet over so that when you start going backward you are heading in the direction you want (fig. B).

6 To steer by moving the back end around, position his head toward the side you want to move away from you. This means that when you want to steer the horse's *left* hind leg over toward the right, you use the reins to position the head to the left, which causes the left hind leg to step over thus changing the direction of the horse's movement. When you need to steer his hind end in the other direction, you will want his *right* hind leg to step over, so position his head toward his right hind leg until he steps over to the left (fig C).

7 Continue asking the horse to back up and step over with his front or hind end until he has completed the whole weave back through the markers.

HOW DO YOU KNOW WHEN YOU'VE DONE IT?

The horse will back up in an even smooth weave through a line of cones.

WHAT YOU CAN DO IF IT DOESN'T HAPPEN

• Don't do too much to start: just one cone will do at first.

• Don't go too fast: Complete one step at a time and think ahead to where you want the horse to go next.

• It's like learning to reverse a trailer: You need to practice. Make mistakes! The only way to learn what works and what doesn't work is to try it.

OTHER THINGS YOU CAN DO WITH THIS EXERCISE

You can back up around corners; in circles; and in figure eights.

A. *Be slow and thoughtful about each footfall as you do this exercise.*

B. *Here, I am moving the front end.*

C. *I am moving the hind end.*

53

REQUIREMENTS

Exercise 52: Back Up While
Weaving through Markers

Feeling for each step in
the backup will help
you keep straight.

HELPFUL HINT

Whenever you want to back
up, just ask—don't demand.
The more demanding and
firm you are the more
likely you will encounter
resistance. Set up the
question and just wait.

Back Up in a Straight Line

WHY DO THIS?

Being able to back your horse in a straight line shows that you can feel each
footfall of the backing up and make the necessary adjustments to maintain
straightness.

HOW TO DO IT

1 The aim of this exercise is to back the horse in a straight line—without him
   resisting and without making exaggerated movements to correct him. In
   other words, you will learn to feel the backing up go awry when "crooked"
   is just a *thought* in your horse's head, before it has reached his feet.
2 Ride the horse forward and halt. Look forward and choose a point in
   front of you to ride *away* from (fig. A).
3 Your energy level is such that you are riding forward, but because the
   horse cannot walk forward due to the feel in your reins, he will go
   backward.
4 Whichever front leg is farther forward (if either) you are going to ask
   that foot to move first. Putting a bit more *feel* into the rein on that side
   (*not* a pull!), ask him to take a step backward. The rein on the other side
   is stopping forward movement, nothing more.
5 After one step, check that you are straight. Has the hind end swung over
   at all? Is the front end beginning to move away from the chosen point
   that you were looking at? If he goes crookedly you will have to reposition him (fig. B).
6 Keep asking for one step at a time while repositioning, if necessary,
   after each one of them.
7 You will start to *feel* when the step is crooked or straight. When the
   step is straight, ask for another straight step. If it is crooked, immediately reposition and ask again. Remember, as his hind end starts to go
   crooked in one direction, turn your horse's head toward that side, and
   the horse will step over to become straight again. Sometimes brushing
   the area behind the girth with your foot on that same side helps.
8 Keep asking and repositioning until you get a straight step, which is
   when you stop: Do not stop if you get a crooked step.

HOW DO YOU KNOW WHEN YOU'VE DONE IT?

The horse will consistently back up in a straight line.

WHAT YOU CAN DO IF IT DOESN'T HAPPEN

• Look for one straight willing step and stop there. This is the essence of
  3-Minute Horsemanship.
• Crookedness is a resistance. Don't fight it; just gently correct.

OTHER THINGS YOU CAN DO WITH THIS EXERCISE

Backing up your horse in a straight line before you ask him to go from halt
straight into canter helps him to engage his hocks and hind end so he's ready
to push off explosively.

A. *Look up at a point and ride back away from it.*

B. *Correct the horse if he starts to get crooked. Here I am moving my horse's near side hind back onto my straight line.*

54

REQUIREMENTS
None

When you can ride on a loose rein it shows you are not using the reins as a brake.

HELPFUL HINT

Make sure your energy level doesn't go up when you loosen the rein. It should stay just the same because that's what you want the horse's energy level to do.

Ride on a Loose Rein

WHY DO THIS?

Having the confidence to let your reins go loose proves to you, and your horse, that they are there for communicating—not braking.

HOW TO DO IT

1 Ride in your usual bridle.
2 Ride at a walk and concentrate on feeling the rhythm. Count footsteps if it helps.
3 When you feel you have a consistent rhythm, release the reins. Do not let them slide, but actually *release* them. You are still holding the reins but they are "on the buckle" (fig. A).
4 Your horse's gait should not change. If it does, then the reins are acting as brakes, which is like driving a vehicle with the brake on all the time.
5 Observe how your horse behaves when he has a longer rein. Does he stretch his neck or shake his head (fig. B)?
6 Gently pick the reins up and ride on.
7 Repeat for longer periods in safe places.

HOW DO YOU KNOW WHEN YOU'VE DONE IT?

The loose rein does not cause the horse to rush ahead.

WHAT YOU CAN DO IF IT DOESN'T HAPPEN

• Only release the rein for one second before picking it up again. Slowly increase the time as the horse gets used to the feeling. Because you are continuing to hold onto the reins, it is easy to pick them up again if you need to stop the horse from rushing ahead.
• Remember, some horses that have always been held tight may find this newfound freedom a chance to relax, so allow them to explore this new feeling.

OTHER THINGS YOU CAN DO WITH THIS EXERCISE

Once you have established this at the walk, you can try this at other gaits.

A. *Let the reins go really loose and ride "on the buckle."*

B. *As the horse becomes more confident you can allow him to begin to stretch right down.*

55

REQUIREMENTS
None

Practicing both upward and downward transitions will teach your horse to give you his attention and be ready to answer your instructions.

HELPFUL HINT

Be consistent with your cues!

25 Transitions

WHY DO THIS?
A transition is a change of gait or pace—not only, for example, walk to trot or trot to canter, but actually within the gait, like a working trot, medium trot, or extended trot. By practicing these changes, you and your horse will begin to have greater understanding of how you both feel and communicate, thus greatly improving the quality of your horsemanship.

HOW TO DO IT
1 These can be done in an arena or out on a trail ride or hack (fig. A).
2 Every few strides ask the horse to change his gait or pace.
3 Choose the transition for which you and your horse are ready. You can go from walk to halt, or trot to canter, or canter to halt. You can change the rhythm of the movement without changing the gait.
4 Just keep changing for three minutes. Aim to make at least 25 transitions.

HOW DO YOU KNOW WHEN YOU'VE DONE IT?
You will find that the horse really starts to listen to you, becoming sharper as he changes gaits.

WHAT YOU CAN DO IF IT DOESN'T HAPPEN
Make sure your cue to change gait or pace is clear and consistent. Give the horse time to feel the request, work out the answer, and reply. The more you do this, the quicker the horse will become at changing.

OTHER THINGS YOU CAN DO WITH THIS EXERCISE
This will really improve your overall horsemanship.

A. *You can practice your transitions outside the arena.*

RIDDEN EXERCISE

56

REQUIREMENTS

Exercise 38: Backing Up;
43: Ride Through a Narrow Gap;
47: Stand in a Narrow Space; and
53: Back Up in a Straight Line

Hone your skills in both backing up and steering the horse backward.

HELPFUL HINT

As with many of these exercises, do not rush this. The aim is for the horse to be relaxed as he goes backward.

Back Up Through a Narrow Gap

WHY DO THIS?

Being able to back your horse through a narrow gap is an exercise in trust and requires both skill in backing up *and* steering.

HOW TO DO IT

1 Make sure the gap you use is safe in case the horse brushes it with his hind end or you do so with your leg. The best thing to use is two plastic barrels that will fall over should the horse rush back. A safe gate is another option.
2 Ensure your horse is relaxed while backing up and that you are not asking him to back up into anything that could scare him, such as an electric fence or another horse.
3 Make sure your horse is calm when walking forward through a narrow space (fig. A).
4 Ride him to halfway through the gap then ask him to back up (fig. B).
5 Continue asking him to walk forward and backward until he is completely through the gap before you ask him to start backing up.
6 Take it one step at a time. If he starts to go crookedly and looks as if he'll bump into the barrels or open gate, just stop, reposition him, and continue backing him (fig. C).

HOW DO YOU KNOW WHEN YOU'VE DONE IT?

The horse will comfortably ride forward through a gap and back up without resistance or fear.

WHAT YOU CAN DO IF IT DOESN'T HAPPEN

• Do not rush this exercise. It is far better to have a horse taking one calm, measured step and stopping, than having him rushing through the gap. A rushing horse is a scared horse.
• If the horse bumps his hind end, don't make a fuss; just reposition him and ask for one good step before finishing the session for that day.

OTHER THINGS YOU CAN DO WITH THIS EXERCISE

Back the horse through the gap without passing forward through it first. Turn him around in front of the gap, then back him through.

A. *Give the horse confidence by riding straight through the narrow gap first.*

B. *Halt halfway through the narrow gap.*

C. *Make sure the way is thoroughly clear before you start backing up.*

RIDDEN EXERCISE

57

REQUIREMENTS
None

"Feel" your horse's next move just before it happens.

Ride in a Straight Line

WHY DO THIS?

To be able to ride your horse at walk in a straight line is an exercise in awareness because you need to *feel* the horse going crookedly when it is just a *thought*—a whisker of an idea—and correct it before anyone sees it happening. This is truly a secret between you and your horse!

HOW TO DO IT

1 This must be done in an open area—not along a wall or fence. Pick two points ahead of you: one marker must be above the other. For example, you can choose a fence post and a tree, or place a cone and a vertical marker, as I have in the photo on the facing page.
2 Place your horse so that you can see these two points between his ears, or above them. This area between his ears is a third point (fig. A).
3 Ride forward at a slow walk and keep the three points in a vertical line: The place between the horse's ears, the fence post, and the tree should all stay one above the other (fig. B).
4 When the points start to go out of line, correct your horse.
5 Finish when the horse is straight even if it happens in fewer than three minutes!

HOW DO YOU KNOW WHEN YOU'VE DONE IT?

The horse will walk straight toward your two points, keeping his poll in line with them.

WHAT YOU CAN DO IF IT DOESN'T HAPPEN

• Start by asking the horse to stand still with the two points positioned between his ears. Take one step. If it is straight, reward him and leave it for the day. Build up the straight steps. When it is solid using your first two points, choose another two in a different place and try again.
• The aim is to feel when the horse is *about to be* crooked and to correct him *before* he is.

OTHER THINGS YOU CAN DO WITH THIS EXERCISE

Ride along roads and tracks in a straight line.

A. *Choose two points and put one above the other between your horse's ears to help keep your focus.*

B. *Concentrate on riding every stride and remaining straight.*

58

REQUIREMENTS

For safety, you must follow the instructions given. Removing the bit and bridle without the necessary training can confuse a horse and make him somewhat fearful.

Riding without the use of the bit demonstrates there is more than one way to communicate.

HELPFUL HINT

Leave the halter reins loose, only using them when you need to ask a question. Otherwise the horse can start leaning on them.

Ride with a Halter and Lead Rope

WHY DO THIS?

This exercise can help prove to you that the bit is for fine communication and how—with support—you can ride without one.

HOW TO DO IT

1 Leave your normal bridle on the horse while you are learning this skill.
2 Put a halter and long lead rope over the bridle. Tie the lead rope in a loop like reins, or attach standard reins to the sides of the halter (fig. A). This will give you two sets of reins for the time being.
3 When you ride your horse in this exercise, you will primarily use the halter reins. But when your horse does not understand, use the reins attached to the bit to communicate your question clearly. Be aware that the communication through the halter may not be as clear as the bit, so don't expect an instant answer to a question when you use the halter rein. Give the horse time to *feel* the question and answer it.
4 Alternate between the two sets of reins as and when you need them (figs. B–D). Tie some cord from D-ring to D-ring on the front of your saddle through which both sets of reins can be looped, so that they are always there, ready to be picked up as you need them.
5 Ride at walk and halt in a small safe enclosure, using just the halter rein, so that you and the horse can get the idea before you go into a larger area. Do not proceed too fast; you are both learning a new means of communication and it takes time to adjust.

HOW DO YOU KNOW WHEN YOU'VE DONE IT?

You are not using the bridle's reins to communicate and your horse responds to the halter reins instead.

WHAT YOU CAN DO IF IT DOESN'T HAPPEN

It may be that your horse is not comfortable with the pressure on his nose from the halter. For older horses who have worn a bit for years, this can be a big change for them. Spend longer just riding your horse out with both halter and bridle.

OTHER THINGS YOU CAN DO WITH THIS EXERCISE

If all you do is learn to appreciate that the bit is not the only means of communicating with your horse, then this is a worthwhile exercise.

A. *The arrangement of halter and bridle.*

B. *Holding both the bridle and halter reins.*

C. *Holding just the bridle reins.*

D. *Holding just the halter reins.*

59

REQUIREMENTS

Exercise 58: Ride with a
Halter and Lead Rope

When you ride without
a bridle, you become
much more aware of how
you use your body to
communicate with the
horse when in the saddle.

HELPFUL HINT

Give your horse time to
answer the question. If he
gives the wrong answer,
don't stop asking. Keep
going until he gives even
a tiny suggestion that he
understands what you are
trying to do.

Ride without Reins

WHY DO THIS?
This exercise shows that the horse is responding to your body's cues and not just rein cues.

HOW TO DO IT
1 Ride in your usual bridle or halter if you have mastered Exercise 58 (p. 126).
2 You are going to go through a pattern every time you want the horse to respond to a body cue. When, at any time, your horse does what you want, then reward immediately.
3 In a safe, small, riding area, hold the reins on the buckle—that is, at their very end (fig. A).
4 Ask the horse to walk on.
5 Now you are going to turn left. Look left with intention that you're going there (fig. B).
6 Turn your body left (fig. C).
7 Put your right leg on the horse's side just in front of the girth.
8 Lift your left rein up and out (fig. D).
9 The horse will look or even turn right. Stop and reward.
10 Reverse these cues to turn in the opposite direction.

HOW DO YOU KNOW WHEN YOU'VE DONE IT?
The horse will turn in the direction you intentionally look toward, without you using the reins.

WHAT YOU CAN DO IF IT DOESN'T HAPPEN
Slow down and keep trying. Make sure you are working through the series of questions listed above and not cutting corners.

OTHER THINGS YOU CAN DO WITH THIS EXERCISE
One day you will be able to take the bridle off altogether and ride your horse using only your body's cues (figs. E–G).

A. *Begin by riding on the buckle with the halter and lead rope.*

B. *To start a turn, I use my eyes first.*

C. *I turn my belly button to face the way I want to go.*

D. *Then, I lift the rein.*

E. *When I take the halter off, I use all the same body language.*

F. *I ask my horse to back up . . .*

G. *. . . and turn left.*

60

REQUIREMENTS

Exercise 38: Backing Up; and 42: Focus Your Riding

Seamlessly change direction with no discernible rein pressure—just a suggestion.

HELPFUL HINT

Don't pull on the reins. Be very quiet in how you "close the front door."

Ride Forward and, without Stopping, Back Up

WHY DO THIS?

This exercise helps with your "stops" and will engage and balance your horse in the halt.

HOW TO DO IT

1 Ride your horse forward in a straight line. It can help to have a barrier ahead of you. Count steps if this helps you to focus (fig. A).
2 Keeping your energy level up, put a little *feel* into the reins to suggest to the horse that the "front door" is now closed. Do not stop riding! All you are doing is changing direction from forward to going backward (figs. B & C).
3 The horse may hesitate or stop. Keep your energy level raised until he takes a slight rock back, he may even take a step. Reward him when he does.

HOW DO YOU KNOW WHEN YOU'VE DONE IT?

The seamlessness when changing direction from going forward to backward will take your breath away.

WHAT YOU CAN DO IF IT DOESN'T HAPPEN

• Ensure that you are not pulling on the reins. The pressure you put into the reins to turn forward into backward should just be a "suggestion."
• Sometimes it's easier to ride straight toward a fence to help with the change to going back. As the horse reaches the solid fence, close your rein and ride back away from the fence.

OTHER THINGS YOU CAN DO WITH THIS EXERCISE

You can use this exercise to engage the hindquarters, causing the front end to become lighter (fig. D).

A. *Ride forward in a straight line—toward a barrier can be helpful.*

B. *When you reach the barrier, change your thinking from forward to backward . . .*

C. *. . . and keep riding. Don't stop!*

D. *Without the barrier, everything should already be in place to maintain your horse's balance and engage his hindquarters.*

REAL LIFE SCENARIOS

Scenarios 1–15

USING *3-MINUTE HORSEMANSHIP* IN REAL LIFE

Now that you've practiced a number of the *3-Minute Exercises*, you will have found that some are easier than others. Many will have been enjoyable and others really challenging. But one thing's for sure, you will have started to build a strong foundation of trust between you and your horse, which will give him the confidence to always try and do as you ask.

It's great fun to be able to carry out a whole pile of interesting tricks and skills with your horse, but it's even nicer to know they're going to be useful later on, too. So let's put the exercises to work to help solve some common problems.

Horse owners, trainers, and riders can be completely overwhelmed when faced with a complex challenge, but it begins to look a lot more manageable when broken down into smaller exercises. Every single *3-Minute Exercise* can be used to solve a much bigger problem. The skill is in knowing which ones to use!

This ability to break down a big task into little pieces isn't difficult, but it takes planning and it takes honesty. You really need to be realistic about where to start. Most of us start with the problem, get into a tangle, and spend more time sorting *that* out than if we'd made a plan that started at the beginning.

Trailer loading is the most obvious example here, which is why it's *Real Life Scenario One*: It shows just how far back at the beginning you need to start. If the horse moves through the early exercises quickly, no time has been wasted, but if you overface him early on, you could spend a lot more time working it out.

There are two ways to come up with a plan:

1 Ask someone who's done it before and follow her advice. This is a great idea if you like her training methods and they work for you and your horse.

But supposing you don't like her plan, or want to do something that no one has worked out and written down anywhere. You might need to move on to the second way.

2 Build your plan by starting with your final goal and work backward. I find if I keep asking myself, "And what do I need to do before I do *that*?" I eventually end up with a list of things I have to do, which leads me to achieving the final goal.

I work in a three layer system:

- I take a sheet of paper and I write my goal at the top.
- I ask myself, "What do I need to do before I do *that*?"
- I write down the tasks needed to reach the goal.

For each task I then ask that same question, "What do I need to do before I do *that*?" and I keep writing the answer to that question on my list.

When I've finished my list I can see that I've written down an easy-to-follow plan. I don't always completely stick to it—things can change while I am working. I am always prepared to adapt and alter it to suit myself and the horse. When it's working, I stick with it, but when it isn't, I stop and have a think about it.

A horseman doesn't work *to a method*—he works *with the horse*.

And yes, you do have enough time!

I was once at an equine fair when a lady came to my booth to ask my advice. She said she was tired of being the last one left on the showground at the end of the day. Her horse would only take 15 minutes to load up at home, but when she wanted to return he could take hours.

I gently suggested that she *train* her horse to load.

"Oh he loads," she remarked, "it just takes a long time."

"Wouldn't it be better if he just walked straight in?" I asked her.

She looked at me a little suspiciously.

"How long would it take me to train him?"

"Three minutes a day," I told her.

"Oh!" She sputtered, "I haven't got time for that!"

I guess that poor lady will spend many more hours on the showground at the end of the day, but for me there is pleasure in actually training horses to load into trailers. Each individual skill required to do it becomes fascinating to me. I love watching the horse learn and try with no force or fear.

So the first *Real Life Scenario*, Trailer Loading, can be the most challenging for some horses because it contains so many skills they need to learn before they are completely comfortable. It is the longest and most complex of exercises. If you can do this one, you are well on the way to being able to do all the others and start to build your own plans. Once you can do this, you can do anything. Just keep asking, "What do I need to do before I do *that*?"

1

Trailer Loading

GOAL: To have your horse walk straight into a trailer, stand quietly while you close everything up, then travel calmly.

This is the longest *Real Life Scenario* because there are so many small parts to the whole task. You will see at the end, however, that if it is done as a collection of *3-Minute Exercises*, the very longest it is going to take you is 60 minutes actual training time, plus time outs. From then on your horse will load in seconds!

WHY DO THIS?

Is there an event in the world that doesn't have some poor soul at the end of the day struggling to get their horse loaded up to go home? It's frustrating and upsetting for everyone, especially the horse. So let's look at the way we are going to make this a stress-free experience for everyone.

HOW TO DO IT

Remember before each task always ask yourself, "What do I need to do before I do *that*?" Look through the following list of *3-Minute Exercises* to help you decide which ones will help you achieve each task. Review them.

Task A: *The horse walks into the trailer.*

> **Exercise 1: Being Still Around a Horse.** The handler needs to stay calm; some horses have an unpleasant association with trailers and become very active.
>
> **Exercise 5: Get a Horse's Attention.** The horse can become very distracted, looking for ways out and not concentrating on you when things get a bit scary. You need to keep his attention on the task if you are to succeed.

Exercise 6: Back Up Away from You. When your horse becomes active, make sure you can move him away from you.

Exercise 9: Invite a Horse to Walk Toward You. The horse must always feel comfortable when walking toward you because you might be inside a trailer, asking him to come to you (fig. A).

Exercise 15: Lead with a Loose Rope. It is impossible to *pull* a horse into a trailer. If you and your horse keep a loose rope between you, he will learn to follow the "feel" of it rather than pulling back against it.

Exercise 16: Move the Front End Over. Sometimes horses get completely stuck in the front, but when you can move those feet, it seems to free the mind. A horse with "loose" feet, even if they are very active, is easier to load than one that is stuck.

Exercise 17: Move the Hind End Over. I find the back feet are often more difficult to load than the front feet. If you can ask the horse to loosen them up, it often frees the horse to move forward toward the trailer (fig. B).

Exercise 21: Walk Forward and Backward a Specific Number of Steps. When you take *your* focus off the trailer and just move backward and forward, this can take the pressure off the horse. He then concentrates on just moving backward and forward, too.

A. *Invite the horse to come to you in the trailer.*

B. *This horse's back feet are "stuck."*

Exercise 23: Place the Front Feet. Forget loading in the trailer—just ask the horse to place a specific foot on a place on the trailer's floor (fig. C). This takes the focus off going in the whole way.

Exercise 24: Place the Hind Feet. This is exactly the same concept as placing the front feet. You will find that every horse has one foot that is harder to move than the others. It can be any foot. When you can identify it early on, focus on freeing it and ask the horse to step onto a mark on the trailer. This often helps all the other feet to become free, too.

Exercise 25: Walk Over Unusual Surfaces. Some horses just cannot cope with a change in surface—even wet to dry pavement—because of the color change! They get used to it, of course, but the floor covering of a trailer can cause a problem. Walk over as many different surfaces as you can so the horse becomes used to constant change. When you get to the trailer, let your horse examine the new surface (fig. D).

Exercise 26: Back Up Over a Pole. This helps your horse to trust you when you are asking him to step back out of the trailer.

Exercise 30: Lead Through a Narrow Gap. You must be certain this exercise can be done quietly—without rushing—before you even think about loading a horse. The "pressure" caused by the sides of a narrow gap can be very threatening.

Task B: *The horse stands still as the trailer is closed up.*

Exercise 2: Measure a Horse's Personal Space. You will be very close to your horse. How comfortable is he with this? He may be more afraid of being in a confined space with *you* than just being in a trailer!

Exercise 3: Calculate Your Personal Space. Are you really ready to train your horse to load? If you are at all concerned or hesitant, your horse will reflect your anxiety.

Exercise 7: Teach Standing Still. Your horse must know that you need him to be still when you ask for it (fig. E).

Exercise 19: Back Up to a Fence. When the ramps or doors are closed behind him the horse must feel secure that his hind end is safe.

Exercise 27: Back Up Between Two Poles. As odd as it seems to us humans, some horses find a ground pole on each side of their body threatening to them. So just imagine how they feel when the pressure of the trailer wall is right up beside their belly!

Exercise 28: Stand Next to a Fence. The horse must feel comfortable when a solid wall or fence is beside his body. When you start to get each side of his body accepting this, it is far easier when you introduce the

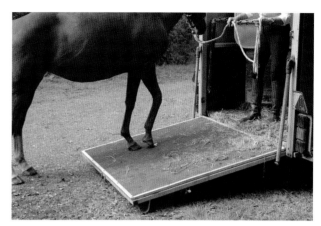

C. *Aim to place each foot on a mark, and forget about loading the horse into the trailer.*

D. *Allow the horse stop and look at a new surface.*

E. *A horse needs to know how to stand still in the trailer.*

trailer's partitions and walls, on both sides at the same time.

Exercise 31: Stand in a Narrow Space. The horse must feel he can stand quite still and be relaxed in a narrow space because that's how he'll be traveling.

Once you have all these *3-Minute Exercises* in place and your horse is happy to stand still, it is time to start closing up the trailer. Do this in stages. Of course, it depends on the design of your trailer, but when there are a number of doors, ramps, and bars to close and bolt, first do each one individually. If these are noisy, get the horse used to the sound when he is *outside* the trailer. This way it won't be such a shock when he first hears the trailer being closed up when he is inside.

So to start, only close each door, or ramp, for a second. The key is to open it up again *before* the horse shows signs of fear. Keep the sessions of opening and closing everything up short and productive. If you leave

F. *The horse should unload quietly and calmly when you ask him.*

him too long and he starts to panic, you will want to get him out of the trailer, of course, but this teaches him that panicky behavior gets him out. So don't let it reach that stage!

If you're not sure how to gauge when things are going wrong, give your horse's behavior a mark out of 10. Give him a score of zero if he is so frightened that he is "climbing out the window" and 10 when he's standing munching his hay in a relaxed state. This is a really good way of helping you make a considered judgment about how ready your horse is to go onto the next thing.

Once you have him standing calmly in the trailer, it's time to get moving.

Task C: *The horse travels calmly.*
The horse is now loaded and calmly standing in the trailer. You want him to stay that way so ensure that you drive with this in mind. Think about smoothly pulling away, steering around corners, and braking as if you have a bucket of water in the back and don't want to spill it!

When your horse has been a very reluctant loader, make that first trip for a few feet only. Yes, just turn on the engine, drive 6 feet (2m) and stop. Wait a second or two and unload your horse. These "journeys" and the wait before you open up the trailer can be made longer as you go on. Essentially, you want the horse to stand quietly when the trailer stops moving because it is not always practical to get him out right away.

Before you unload, untie him and drape the rope safely over his neck: Should he start to unload himself when you open the door or ramp and finds he is tied, he may panic and pull back. It is better to allow him to exit if he rushes to unload but *immediately* load him up again; ask him to stand and wait, until *you* ask him to unload (fig. F).

The *3-Minute Exercises* you need to train your horse to load easily are Exercises 1, 2, 3, 5, 6, 7, 9, 15, 16, 17, 19, 21, 23, 24, 25, 26, 27, 28, 30, and 31. This is 20 times 3 minutes—60 minutes overall—plus time in between. Now just think how many hours you can spend trying to load a difficult horse. . . . A lot more than that!

HOW DO YOU KNOW WHEN YOU'VE DONE IT?
Your horse walks straight into the trailer, stands quietly while you close everything up, and then he travels calmly.

WHAT YOU CAN DO IF IT DOESN'T HAPPEN
You have gone too fast. Every challenge has a solution when you are prepared to *take the time that it takes* (figs. G–K).

G. *Even if the horse only looks at the trailer, reward him!*

H. *When your horse is afraid of the ramp, try walking him over it from one side to the other.*

I. *Hang out around the trailer; make it a pleasant place outside . . .*

J. *. . . and inside.*

K. *Eventually your horse should load himself!*

2 Opening and Closing a Gate

GOAL: To smoothly and efficiently open, ride through and close a gate without letting go of the gate.

Being able to open and close gates from the horse is easy when you practice the individual skills to do so. It is an ideal use of *3-Minute Exercises* because the series of events needed to make this quick and simple are all easy to do and build up into a very useful skill.

WHY DO THIS?

Not having to get on and off your horse to open gates makes life so much easier!

HOW TO DO IT

Task A: *On foot, work out what you are going to do.*
Walk through the maneuver without the horse. When the gate opens *toward* you, hold onto it; back up pulling the gate open toward you; turn around the end of the gate; back up through the gap then keep backing up to pull it closed. When the gate opens *away* from you, open it by pushing; pass through the opening before turning around the end of the gate; then walk toward the gate while pushing it to close.

Task B: *Open the gate on horseback.*
Review the following exercises:

> **Exercise 38: Backing Up.** This will have to be done with the reins in one hand because the other will be holding the gate.
> **Exercise 42: Focus Your Riding.** Be very aware of each stage: Do not see this task as a whole but as individual movements that when done together mean you can open and close a gate.
> **Exercise 49: Walk Forward and Backward a Specific Number of Steps** This focuses your mind on controlling the distance covered as you move through the gate. Many horses rush through so that you have to let go of the gate.
> **Exercise 40: Move the Hind End Over.** You will need this as you turn your horse around the end of the gate.

Exercise 43: Ride Through a Narrow Gap. Your horse should be very calm as you ask him to pass through the gap or you may end up with your leg squashed against the gate or the post if he rushes.

Exercise 56: Back Up Through a Narrow Gap. If you need to draw the gate toward you to close it your horse will need to back up while you are holding it. The horse should wait until you have him in position before he backs up, otherwise he could back into the gate post and hurt himself, or drag your leg against it as he passes through.

HOW DO YOU KNOW WHEN YOU'VE DONE IT?

You will be able to open, pass through and close a gate while riding (figs. A–D).

WHAT YOU CAN DO IF IT DOESN'T HAPPEN

Practice each individual *3-Minute Exercise* again. You will find that one is not quite solid enough. Work on that one, then open and close the gate taking only one step at a time, sitting still and quietly between each step. The aim is not to get the horse and you through the gate any old way: The aim is to achieve a *smooth transition* through the gate without rushing.

HELPFUL HINTS

- **Do not take your hand off the gate while you are carrying out this maneuver!**

- **Choose a gate that swings freely for practice.**

A–D. *Opening and closing a gate on horseback.*

3 Catching a Horse

GOAL: To have your horse come to you in the pasture and stand quietly and softly while you put the halter on.

It is strange that we talk about "catching" a horse but we don't talk about "catching" a dog. This *Real Life Scenario* is about helping the horse to learn that when he is with you, he is in a good place.

WHY DO THIS?

There is nothing more frustrating than getting ready to do something with your horse, and he decides he doesn't want to be caught. When a horse doesn't allow himself to be caught, he's giving you feedback. It may be that he doesn't like coming in because the work is too hard, the grass is too delicious, or he just doesn't know what he's supposed to do. We need to show the horse that coming to his owner to have his halter put on is a pleasant experience.

HOW TO DO IT

Task A: *Get your horse's attention.*
Your horse will need to know that you are trying to communicate with him before you even start. These *3-Minute Exercises* will help him realize that you need his attention, even when he is in a field full of grass and other horses.

> **Exercise 2: Measure a Horse's Personal Space.** Your horse may not be comfortable around human beings; you may have to work on this in a smaller area first.
> **Exercise 3: Calculate Your Personal Space.** How confident are you about going into a field where your horse and maybe many others are grazing? If you feel uncomfortable, it may well make the horse unsure, too.
> **Exercise 5: Get a Horse's Attention.** You need to make yourself more interesting than to him than grass and friends! Once you have this exercise established, you will have

HELPFUL HINT

If the horse looks away as you approach him, he could well be thinking of taking off. Stop walking and turn away but keep half an eye on him. The stop often causes him to turn back to you and reconsider. Wait for him to relax before you continue.

to do less and less to gain his attention because he will want to be with you (fig. A).

Task B: *Ask him to walk toward you.*
The body language is very important here. You will be inviting your horse to walk to you into your personal space so you need to know how to ask the horse to come toward you, as well as make sure he knows where and when to stop.

> **Exercise 9: Invite a Horse to Walk Toward You.** Make sure you are in the correct place and using the right body language or the horse will not want to come to you. Although this exercise uses the lead rope, if you practice your position and body language enough, the horse will follow these signals when there is no rope attached.

Task C: *Stand quietly while you put the halter on.*
The horse must be still and at peace as you "capture" him. When he is part of this process he will be much easier to handle as you lead him in from the pasture.

> **Exercise 1: Being Still Around a Horse.** Once you and the horse are closer together you need to make sure you maintain a sense of calm or your horse may feel concerned and leave before you have put on the halter.
> **Exercise 6: Back Up Away from You.** It may seem strange that you need this skill when you've just spent time teaching him to come *to* you! Whenever your horse is on a lead rope or loose in the field with you, make sure you can keep him away from you, should he suddenly become active.
> **Exercise 7: Teach Standing Still.** The horse needs to stand still while you put on the halter. Make sure you have this ready so he is not waiting for you to sort the halter out, or he may have second thoughts and leave before you have secured him.
> **Exercise 11: Lower the Head.** Even a tiny child can put a halter on a draft horse as long as the horse has been

taught to lower his head. But when the horse turns into a giraffe instead, you need to work on lowering his head first.

Exercise 12: Bend the Head Around to the Side. Whenever you go to get your horse, make sure he is part of the catching process by asking him to bring his head down and around to you.

HOW DO YOU KNOW WHEN YOU'VE DONE IT?

Your horse acknowledges you when you enter the pasture and comes to you to have his halter put on.

WHAT YOU CAN DO IF IT DOESN'T HAPPEN

Think about your body language. Are you moving too fast? Are you approaching the horse from the wrong angle? It is far better to wander in a half circle toward your horse than walk straight toward him. Make sure the catching area isn't too big. It is easier to work on this *Real Life Scenario* in a small yard or paddock than in a huge field, maybe with other horses there, too.

A. *Ask yourself, why wouldn't your horse want to be with you?*

4

Leading a Horse Reluctant to Move

GOAL: To be able to lead your horse anywhere, on a loose rope, without dragging him behind you.

Horses can be very good at sticking their feet into the ground and refusing to move. Unfortunately some people think that horses can be pulled along like a trolley, but all this does is cause him to pull back into the pressure, slowing him down. When you lead your horse the process should feel smooth and easy, almost as if the lead rope isn't there.

WHY DO THIS?

A horse that moves with you wherever you go on a loose rope is a joy to handle (fig. A).

HOW TO DO IT

Task A: *Establish a signal that means "Walk."*
Review the following exercises:

Exercise 2: Measure a Horse's Personal Space. He may be frightened to move because you are too close.
Exercise 5: Get a Horse's Attention. He may not want to walk because the grass or his friends are more interesting than you.
Exercise 9: Invite a Horse to Walk Toward You. Make sure you are not looking at him directly in the eye. This can often stop a horse from coming to you.
Exercise 10: Synchronize Movement. Be sure you are moving freely and with intent.
Exercise 15: Lead with a Loose Rope. The horse needs to know he is meant to follow the feel on the lead rope. The

---

HELPFUL HINT

Be consistent and look for one step at a time. It's easy to give up and get frustrated. Remember it never takes longer than *three minutes*!

---

key to this *Real Life Scenario* is to look for one relaxed willing step—and reward. Then ask for another step and so on.

Task B: *Establish a signal that means "Stop."*

Exercise 7: Teach Standing Still. The horse needs to know that it is safe to stand still with you and sometimes, that you expect it of him (fig. B).

Task C: *Figure out a strategy to move the horse's feet.*

Exercise 16: Move the Front End Over. This frees the front feet when they are stuck.
Exercise 17: Move the Hind End Over. You free up the hind feet.

HOW DO YOU KNOW WHEN YOU'VE DONE IT?

You are able to lead your horse anywhere, on a loose rope, without dragging him.

WHAT YOU CAN DO IF IT DOESN'T HAPPEN

Make sure your body language and cues are consistent. Often, I see people leaning backward, which they have already taught the horse means, "Back up." Meanwhile they are signaling with their hand for the horse to go forward. The horse doesn't know which signal to respond to—the hand or the leaning back—so he does nothing.

A. *A horse should be able to be quietly led on a loose rope—anywhere.*

B. *Make sure your horse also understands "Stop."*

5

Stop a Horse from Barging Into You

GOAL: To lead the horse on a loose rope without him pushing into you with any part of his body.

Many horses use their shoulder or body to push you out of the way. This could be because they are afraid and have become unaware of their handler in their bid to escape, or they want to get closer to you so they feel safer. Sometimes it is a learned technique, which means *they* are trying to move *you* by choosing the speed and direction of the movement.

WHY DO THIS?

This is a safety issue. A horse that uses his body in this way is capable of seriously hurting a human. It is also important the horse understands that the handler is in charge of *how* and *where* they are both going.

HOW TO DO IT

Task A: *Lead the horse on a loose rope.*
When the lead rope between you and the horse is loose it gives him the opportunity to look after his own balance and allows him to feel less claustrophobic.

> **Exercise 15: Lead with a Loose Rope.** Establish this exercise first in a safe quiet place where the horse is unlikely to barge into you to teach him the rules of correct leading so that when and if he starts to barge he already knows how you want him to behave.

Task B: *Create a safe personal space around you*
Know how to quietly and assertively protect yourself so that if the horse starts to run into you, you are able to respond.

> **Exercise 2: Measure a Horse's Personal Space.** As I said above, some horses try to get closer to their handler when they are scared. This is not a safe option for you so make sure he knows that pushing into your space at *any time* is unacceptable (fig. A).
>
> **Exercise 3: Calculate Your Personal Space.** Are you capable of training this type of horse to lead? If you step away or hesitate when he starts this behavior, you will actually make it worse. All your energy must be sent toward the horse to move him away from you—if it is safe to do so.
>
> **Exercise 6: Back Up Away from You.** Have the signal to back away solidly understood by the horse—so solid that

even when he is really trying to run into you, he will respond to your request to back away.

> **Exercise 7: Teach Standing Still.** When the horse is pushing into you, you might need to be quite "big" with your body language, but as soon as he has moved away, the best thing to do is to stay still so that he sees a definite change in energy level from you.

Task C: *Have a strategy if the horse tries to barge into you.*
Although you might be able to lead your horse on a loose rope, you do need to know how to create a safe distance should the horse start pushing into your personal space (figs. B–D).

> **Exercise 5: Get a Horse's Attention.** You may need to make yourself pretty "noisy" and big to ensure the horse knows you are there. As soon as he acknowledges you, first ask him to back away, then be still.
>
> **Exercise 12: Bend the Head Around to the Side.** This action "shapes" his body to be able to step his hind end away.
>
> **Exercise 16: Move the Front End Over.** "Read" the horse so you can see what he's going to do long before it becomes "big" and dangerous. What does he do before he barges into you? Toss his head, look away and push his cheek toward you (the shoulder will follow this), or does he simply just lean in your direction? A horse always does something before he barges, so get good at seeing it coming; you can deal with the small thing first.

HELPFUL HINT

Barging can be a really ingrained habit in some horses. Consistency is the key here. Your horse has to earn the right to be allowed into your personal space. Even something as small as the horse leaning into you at halt can be the start of a full-scale barge.

HOW DO YOU KNOW WHEN YOU'VE DONE IT?

You can lead your horse on a loose rope without him pushing into you with any part of his body.

WHAT YOU CAN DO IF IT DOESN'T HAPPEN

Slow down and start to look for the small things. Ask a friend to video a walk with your horse so you can see what the horse does before he barges. Look for a pattern so that you can begin to read what is about to happen and deal with it before the big stuff occurs!

A. *Keep a safe distance between you and a lively horse.*

B. *You can do something about it when you can see the barge about to happen.*

C. *This horse, Ziggy, always tosses his head before he barges.*

D. *Clancy walks toward Ziggy to move him away from her.*

6

Stop a Horse from Biting

GOAL: To train your horse to stop biting people.

Being bitten by a horse is a painful and often frightening experience. Biting is a habit that needs to be stopped before it causes serious injury. However, before you start to deal with it, you need to ask yourself: Is the horse trying to tell me he's in pain; is it just a habit; or is he trying to play?

WHY DO THIS?

A bite from a horse can cause serious injury so you must prevent it from happening.

HOW TO DO IT

Task A: *Find out what is causing the horse to bite.*
There are five main reasons why a horse bites his handler (see p. 147 for solutions):

1 *Pain.* He's trying to tell you something hurts when you do a specific action. For example, he may bite when you put the saddle on because it is causing him pain (fig. A).

2 *Habit.* Biting a person becomes a habit. It can occur when food is involved: The horse is given food and when he has finished he will often nuzzle or nip to look for more. If the human gives the horse more food, she rewards the behavior. This nip can soon become a bite.

3 *Play.* If you watch horses play, they often nip and bite each other without any signs of injury; your horse may be trying to initiate play by giving you a nip. He doesn't mean to hurt you, but because he's a horse he doesn't understand that humans are more fragile than he is.

4 *Fear.* The horse may be afraid and feels he needs to defend himself. Given a choice a horse will move away from something frightening, but when he feels he has no way to escape he may attack with his teeth before turning to kick out.

5 *Trying to move you around.* When a horse is trying to tell another horse to move away he asks quietly at first, building up the pressure until the demand becomes quite "loud." For example, he may just "make a face" at first; then move forward; then bite. It may appear quite savage but as I mentioned, a horse biting another rarely causes serious injury.

Note: Just because your horse bites other horses, it doesn't mean he'll bite humans.

Task B: *Set up a strategy to train the horse to stop biting.*
Once you know what is causing the biting to happen you can start to deal with it. The *3-Minute Exercises* you need to have in place here before you even get started are:

Exercise 1: Being Still Around a Horse. Some horses don't like you to be showing high energy, so learn to be calm and unemotional. When a horse bites you it is not a planned, vindictive attack, he's simply communicating with you.

Exercise 2: Measure a Horse's Personal Space. Your horse might be warning you to stay away.

Exercise 3: Calculate Your Personal Space. Do not attempt to train a serious biter. The bite can be there in a flash, and sometimes it is very difficult to see it coming. And when the horse bites you and you move away, he's just learned that biting can be used to move you around and control your feet.

Exercise 6: Back Up Away from You. When a horse isn't too close to you, he can't bite you. With a confirmed biter, keep him far enough away from you when you handle him so that he cannot reach you with his teeth! Sometimes handling such an animal in this way causes the biting to become extinct over a period of time. In other words, the horse "forgets" that biting worked to get what he wanted, so he stops doing it.

HELPFUL HINT

Only feed treats to your horse if you absolutely know that you can back him away from you when you have a treat in your hand. Then *you* go to the *horse* and give it to him; he should *never* take it from you.

Here again are the five main causes of biting with some suggestions to help you deal with the problem.

1 *Pain.* When you think this is the issue behind the biting behavior, look for a pattern. Does the horse only bite when you put the saddle on; touch him on his neck; or when you try and pick up a foot? He could be telling you that it hurts when you do any of these things. Get good professional advice to get rid of the pain. However, by that time the biting may have become a habit (see below) so you will need to change your approach slightly.

   One of my horses had an ill-fitting saddle in the past and although he was physically well with a good saddle, he would still turn his head to bite me when I tried to do up the girth. I reacted by telling him I was displeased, but it made no difference, so I started to do the complete opposite: Whenever he turned to bite me, I stroked his face and made a fuss of him. He soon learned that having the saddle put on and girthed up was a pleasant experience and the biting stopped.

2 *Habit.* Keep the horse far enough away so that he can't reach you; eventually he may forget that biting works. Do not invite him to come to you for treats.

3 *Play.* The last thing you want to do is shut your horse down by telling him he can't play, but he does need to realize that play biting is *not* tolerated by human beings. Getting this message across is tricky: One way that *doesn't* work is hitting him when he bites. He'll just see that as you joining in the game, and if you get the timing wrong he can get confused by your action and possibly become head shy and afraid of you.

   The following method is used by a friend of mine who runs an equine rescue center: As soon as a horse bites her, she screams out loud and jumps up and down! She doesn't look at the horse or touch him. He just learns that biting a human initiates a rather horrible noise and soon stops.

4 *Fear.* A horse that feels trapped or frightened will use everything he can to keep himself safe. Training the bite out of this horse is a long process requiring a lot of patience. It's no use getting mad or punishing him for his actions because he already has a strategy to deal with this—he bites! When you need to handle a horse like this you can manage the behavior by keeping him away from you, or you can pad your arms, body, and wear a face shield to protect yourself! That means that when he bites, he doesn't get a response from you—you can just ignore the

bite and get on with your work. This often works wonders but is not for the fainthearted!

5 *Trying to move you around.* Horses are masters at moving other horses around, and they will often use the same techniques on humans—to good effect. Horses are so big and strong it is easy for them to drag their handler about. But when the handler is "in the way" the horse will sometimes bite to get her to move. It's not vicious, it's just "horse talk," but he must learn it doesn't work with humans. Get good at moving your horse's feet. Many of the *3-Minute Exercises* will help you take charge of his feet, but what's even more important is that the horse must be aware that *he* is *not* in charge of *your* feet.

All the following *Exercises* will help you take charge of your horse's feet:

> Exercise 16: Move the Front End Over
> Exercise 17: Move the Hind End Over
> Exercise 18: Move a Horse Sideways
> Exercise 34: Change Direction While Not Moving Your Feet
> Exercise 35: Turn Using a Rope Over the Hocks

HOW DO YOU KNOW WHEN YOU'VE DONE IT?

You will feel safe around your horse because you either know he no longer bites or you have a strategy for dealing with it.

WHAT YOU CAN DO IF IT DOESN'T HAPPEN

Seek a professional trainer's help.

A. *A horse may bite when you put on the saddle or girth up because it causes him pain.*

7 Standing for Foot Handling

GOAL: The horse stands quietly while his feet are given attention.

A horse that won't stand still to have his feet trimmed or shod is a danger to the farrier and himself. If you can help him come to terms with remaining still on three legs while someone (maybe a stranger) prevents his escape, you are well on the way to building a strong positive relationship with your horse.

WHY DO THIS?

This is one of the foundation skills a domestic horse must learn if you are to keep his feet in good condition (fig. A).

HOW TO DO IT

Task A: *The horse must stand still.*
Some horses don't know that it is safe to stand still around people. Teach your horse to stand and relax before you start to try and pick up his feet.

> **Exercise 1: Being Still Around a Horse** You need to stay calm because some horses start moving around when asked to give a foot for treatment.
> **Exercise 7: Teach Standing Still.** Your horse must feel safe while standing still in the presence of both familiar people and strangers.

Task B: *The horse accepts that you can move his feet.*
The simplest way of doing this is to show him that when you do move his feet, no harm comes to him.

> **Exercise 15: Lead with a Loose Rope**
> **Exercise 16: Move the Front End Over**
> **Exercise 17: Move the Hind End Over**

Task C: *Acceptance of the legs being touched.*
Horses instinctively dislike having strange things touch their legs: When a horse's leg becomes trapped in the wild, making it impossible for him to run away, he will not survive. So, be quietly respectful as you handle his legs, showing him that you have no intention of hurting him.

> **Exercise 2: Measure a Horse's Personal Space.** The horse's legs are his running-away mechanism! If he feels they might become trapped—or injured—he will feel he needs to do something about it.

Exercise 12: Bend the Head Around to the Side. From this position, if the horse threatens to kick out, you will be able to pull his head toward you, thus sending his hind end away.

Note: I also use a padded stick to help the horse get used to the feeling of something strange touching his legs. Using this means that if he does kick out he will only kick the stick and not me. If I didn't use the padded stick and he kicked me, I would likely move away, showing him that kicking works! But when he kicks the padded stick, I can just keep on touching his legs (fig. B).

He will pretty soon learn that kicking doesn't work; it doesn't get rid of the strange object touching him, so he will stop trying it. Once he has accepted the stick all over the inside and outside of his legs, you can begin to work your own hand down to the stick until your hand is touching him instead of the stick (fig. C).

A. *A horse must learn to stand quietly while a farrier tends to his feet.*

Task D: *Acceptance of a foot being restrained.*

Make sure the horse is standing square so that he can balance on three legs. Most horses that don't accept a foot being held up are moving about because they feel they are going to fall down. Give your horse time to find his balance before you start trying to hold his foot up for any length of time.

You want to avoid the horse learning that kicking gets rid of people. So I use a long soft rope looped around the fetlock to lift the foot at first, accompanied by a vocal cue of, "Foot up" (figs. D–F).

If the horse pulls his foot away after he has lifted it, I am still in control: I can immediately ask for the foot again, reward him, and put the foot down without him pulling it away from me. I only hold the foot up for a fraction of a second before I put it down. If he snatches the foot away, I ask for it again immediately and make sure I replace it on the ground.

HOW DO YOU KNOW WHEN YOU'VE DONE IT?

Your horse stands quietly while his feet are given attention.

WHAT YOU CAN DO IF IT DOESN'T HAPPEN

Take more time to accustom your horse to strange sensations around his legs and feet. Only pick his foot up for one second before you put it down. And, do not expect your farrier to train your horse; this is not his job.

B. *I am using a padded stick to help this wild pony get used to having his legs touched, within hours of being first haltered.*

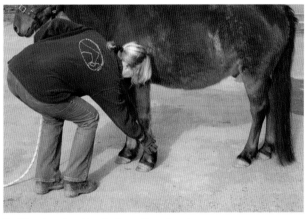

C. *Now, I am touching the legs with my hand.*

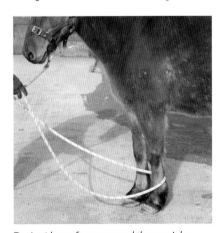

D. *I guide a soft rope around the pony's leg . . .*

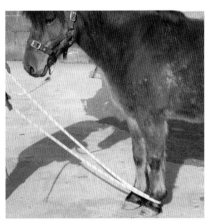

E. *. . . and put a little pressure on it below the fetlock.*

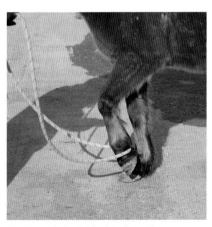

F. *When the leg is lifted, I release the rope.*

8 Standing to Be Mounted

GOAL: The horse must stand quite still as you mount, and wait until he is instructed to move off.

Many people think it is normal to be halfway mounted when the horse moves off. This is quite unnecessary—and dangerous. Every horse can be taught to stand quietly as the rider gets on.

WHY DO THIS?

This is necessary for safety, as well as to demonstrate that the horse has accepted the rider.

HOW TO DO IT

Task A: *The horse must stand still.*
Make sure the horse is absolutely solid with this task before you move on to the next one. And if you are using one, he should be standing still and close to the mounting block (fig. A). Horses are expert at teaching people that they won't—or don't—stand close to the mounting block!

> **Exercise 1: Being Still Around a Horse.** You must behave as if you have all day to wait until the horse becomes comfortable when standing still next to the mounting block.
> **Exercise 2: Measure a Horse's Personal Space.** Before you get on, ensure your horse is happy with you near him on the ground and when you are on the mounting block.
> **Exercise 7: Teach Standing Still**
> **Exercise 28: Stand Next to a Fence**
> **Exercise 29: Stand Still at the Mounting Block**

You need to be able to reposition the horse if he moves. The exercise list below seems like a very long one but you may not need all of them. The ones that involve moving the horse forward, backward, right, and left ensure that you can easily reposition him if he moves away.

When he moves away from the mounting block, immediately reposition him and start again. This has got to be *immediate* or you will give the horse what horseman Mark Rashid calls an "inadvertent reward." In other words, the horse thinks he's done the right thing by moving away because he is not corrected within two seconds.

Exercise 6: Back Up Away from You
Exercise 8: Back Up a Horse While Beside Him
Exercise 9: Invite a Horse to Walk Toward You
Exercise 15: Lead with a Loose Rope
Exercise 16: Move the Front End Over
Exercise 17: Move the Hind End Over
Exercise 18: Move a Horse Sideways
Exercise 21: Walk Forward and Backward a Specific Number of Steps
Exercise 34: Change Direction While Not Moving Your Feet

Tasks B & C: *The horse must accept the sight of the handler above him and his putting a foot in the stirrup.*
You may need to spend some time grooming or rubbing your horse as you stand above him; make sure you do this on both sides. Lift your leg up as if you are going to get on but don't actually mount. If you want the horse to be really solid, and it is safe to do so, you could jump up and down and wave your arms about!

> **Exercise 12: Bend the Head Around to the Side.** The horse may not be comfortable seeing you suddenly higher than his own ears. So flex the horse's head toward you and make yourself a good place to be.

HELPFUL HINT

You can ask a friend to hold your horse while you get on. The person on the ground can correct the horse while the rider waits on the block for the horse to be moved back to her. This can really help to speed up the timing of the correction, which needs to be almost immediately employed. As the horse gets the idea, he will begin to become happier standing quietly at the mounting block.

Task D: *The horse stands as the rider settles into the saddle.* The horse should not move off until the rider tells him to do so. Be consistent about this: Don't let him move one day and not the next. Take time to settle into the saddle before you move off—on every occasion.

Exercise 36: Teach a Horse to Stand Still

Exercise 37: Flex the Head Around to the Side. When done from the saddle, this movement demonstrates that your horse is relaxed and accepting of you as a rider.

Exercise 49: Walk Forward and Backward a Specific Number of Steps. If the horse moves just after you mount, ride him straight back to the place beside the mounting

block and halt there. He must learn that he should remain there until you ask him to move off.

HOW DO YOU KNOW WHEN YOU'VE DONE IT?
The horse stands quite still as you mount and waits until he is instructed to move off.

WHAT YOU CAN DO IF IT DOESN'T HAPPEN
Look for the small "tries" here. Some horses just do not know they are supposed to stand still as the rider mounts, so take time to show yours that's what you want. And make the mounting area a quiet, pleasant place to be.

A. *Your horse should stand still while you mount from the ground or from a mounting block—whichever side you are mounting from.*

9 Crossing Unusual Surfaces

GOAL: For your horse to cross from one surface to another with confidence.

Horses are naturally suspicious of surfaces that look different and unusual. But when they are allowed to explore and test a new surface, they soon become confident and trust their handler or rider that it is safe.

WHY DO THIS?

To have a horse that will confidently move from one surface to another creates a smoother, more forward horse that is happy to go across water, snow, or manmade surfaces without a fuss (fig. A). If you wish to move efficiently along trails and roads, this is imperative.

HOW TO DO IT

Task A: *The horse must lead easily.*
The following *3-Minute Exercises* are worth completing because they will help you to direct your horse's feet easily without feeling any resistance.

> **Exercise 6: Back Up Away from You**
> **Exercise 7: Teach Standing Still**
> **Exercise 9: Invite a Horse to Walk Toward You**
> **Exercise 15: Lead with a Loose Rope**
> **Exercise 16: Move the Front End Over**
> **Exercise 17: Move the Hind End Over**

Task B: *The horse must see many different surfaces and be shown they are safe to cross.*
The following exercises are useful when you are actually at the unusual surface because you are being more particular about where you are placing the horse's feet, rather than just moving them around in general.

> **Exercise 1: Being Still Around a Horse.** It's possible your horse could become quite active in these situations so you need to remain calm and wait for him to relax.
> **Exercise 23: Place the Front Feet**
> **Exercise 24: Place the Hind Feet**
> **Exercise 25: Walk Over Unusual Surfaces.** The skills in this exercise about approaching and crossing new surfaces quietly will really help here.

Task C. *Ride the horse across different footing.*

> **Exercise 42: Focus Your Riding.** When you ride over an unusual surface, look ahead so you are focusing away from the ground. Pick a point on the horizon and ride toward it; this will encourage the horse to *think forward.*
> **Exercise 44: Ride Over Unusual Surfaces.** This will help you understand what your horse might do when he is uncertain about the footing ahead. Some horses just stop while others turn quickly and flee. When you know what he is likely to do, you can do something about it before it happens.
> **Exercises 50 and 51: Place the Front and Hind Feet.** When your horse is finding it difficult when you are riding him, forget about the surface and place *one* of your horse's feet on a "mark" on the surface. We often become fixated on crossing the entire surface, but really, if we just take one step at a time, we will get there in the end.

Task D: *Change the pace onto, over, and off surfaces.*
Once your horse is confidently crossing each surface at a walk, you can increase the pace. You could trot and canter over it (when safe) or even halt on it. As your horse begins to learn that you are confident about crossing over and through all this different footing, he will start to trust you. Once you have reached this level you can start to jump into and out of water.

HELPFUL HINT

Make sure that any surface really is safe before you ask your horse to go onto it or jump into it. Remember, some footing is absolutely fine when dry but difficult to stand up on when wet.

HOW DO YOU KNOW WHEN YOU'VE DONE IT?

Your horse will cross from one surface to another at any pace and with confidence.

WHAT YOU CAN DO IF IT DOESN'T HAPPEN

You need to go much more slowly. The common problem is that the horse will work well on different footing when he is being lead but when the rider gets on, he refuses to cross. This is usually because the handler always had the horse *follow* her, which of course doesn't happen when you are on his back. When on the ground, you may need to start leading him from his shoulder, or even farther back, so that the horse realizes that he can do this without you in front!

A. *Crossing a narrow wooden bridge, steadily and calmly.*

10 "Spook" Busting

GOAL: To feel safe and confident riding or leading your horse anywhere.

Being able to take your horse out for a ride or walk anywhere takes the worry out of planning your daily horse-related activities.

WHY DO THIS?

Horses that continually spook are a danger to themselves and their rider. We want to keep a certain level of spookiness in our horses but not to the point where they run away at the slightest rustle in the trees. A horse will instinctively shy, but when properly trained, he will soon stop and carry on his way.

HOW TO DO IT

Note: It is advisable to use a longer rope—12 feet (4 m)—when working on the ground here so that if the horse gets active you can stay safely out of the way. But, remember, the key is *not* to let him get *too* active!

Task A: *Be able to lead your horse.*

Exercise 6: Back Up Away from You. When a horse becomes overactive you want him to have room to move without jumping onto you.
Exercise 12: Bend the Head Around to the Side. Keep the horse's head bent around *to you* so should he spook, it will be *away* from you. When he is looking *away* from you, he is more likely to swing his hind end toward you.
Exercise 15: Lead with a Loose Rope
Exercise 20: Lead from the Off Side. You may need to change sides when leading your horse so that *you* are next to the scary object. This means that should the horse spook *away* from it, you will be out of the way.
Exercise 30: Lead Through a Narrow Gap. Horses want space to move in when they are afraid. This isn't always possible. Show your horse that being in a narrow space is quite safe even though he cannot move as freely as he would like.

Task B: *Cope when your horse spooks.*

Exercise 1: Being Still Around a Horse
Exercise 2: Measure a Horse's Personal Space
Exercise 3: Calculate Your Personal Space
Exercise 5: Get a Horse's Attention. Keep your horse's attention on you so that he can see how calm you are.
Exercise 11: Lower the Head. Lowering your horse's head will often lower his adrenaline.
Exercise 14: Throw a Rope Over the Horse's Head. I call this a "controlled" spook! It gets your horse used to things flying over his head.

Task C: *Ride your horse past scary things, knowing that he will listen to you and remain calm.*

Exercise 36: Teach a Horse to Stand Still. Even though you may be riding past the scary object, you need to remain still and calm without grabbing onto the horse and becoming tight (fig. A). Remember to breathe!
Exercise 37: Flex the Head Around to the Side. This helps you keep the horse listening to you and ensures he remains soft in his neck and poll.

HELPFUL HINT

Start small. Do not approach your horse with a large flapping flag on Day One. Fold the flag into a small square to start with and slowly unfold it while the horse learns that it is safe. *Horse Agility* really helps horses to become calm and accepting of spooky objects (fig. B).

Exercise 42: Focus Your Riding. Look past the scary object and ride forward.

Exercise 43: Ride Through a Narrow Gap. Your horse must feel confident that he can still move freely even when the space he is in feels claustrophobic.

Exercise 48: Throw a Rope Over a Horse's Head. As with Ground Exercise 14, the horse will get used to things flying over his head.

Exercise 54: Ride on a Loose Rein. Our instinct is to tighten our reins to stop the horse spooking, but often this just makes the situation worse. Maintain an even supporting contact on the reins so the horse does not feel under additional pressure.

HOW DO YOU KNOW WHEN YOU'VE DONE IT?

You will feel safe and confident riding or leading your horse anywhere.

WHAT YOU CAN DO IF IT DOESN'T HAPPEN

Go more slowly and look for smaller signs of fear or uncertainty in your horse. Put yourself in his position. If you are frightened of spiders you would not get braver if someone forced you to hold a large, hairy tarantula! Start with very small spooky things, or be a long way from them to start with, and build up very slowly. Never push the horse to the point where his fear goes down to his feet and he wants to leave.

A. *Pauline allows Topaz to look at the "scary" flags*

B. *Lesley and Bella are Horse Agility competitors, and this has really helped improve their safety when out riding.*

11 "Napping": Refusing to Leave Home or Other Horses

Goal: To ride your horse confidently away from home and other horses.

When your horse confidently leaves the barn or yard and other horses, it shows that he is able to do the work you ask of him and that he feels his rider will support him should he need it.

WHY DO THIS?

You want to be able to take your horse out for a ride anytime (fig. A). Being unable to move out of your yard is frustrating and, when the horse is very energetic in his bid to return home it can be dangerous.

Note: You need to be honest with yourself about why your horse may not want to go out:

- He may be in pain—check this out first.
- Have you taken the time to build a positive relationship with this horse?
- Are the rides hard work for him and not enjoyable? Is his management suitable for the amount of work you are expecting him to do?
- Is it a habit—a learned response that has worked in the past? If so, you need to break the pattern.
- Do *you* really want to go out for a ride? I'll leave you to answer that one!

HOW TO DO IT

Task A: *Be able to lead your horse.*
Start working on some of the *Ground Exercises*. Don't worry, you won't be walking miles! All you are going to do here is make sure that *you* are in charge of your horse's feet and you are directing them where you want them to go.

> **Exercise 5: Get a Horse's Attention.** Do this away from the barn and the other horses.
> **Exercise 6: Back Up Away from You.** Some horses will try and run into the handler to get back to where they want to go.

The following exercises make sure that the horse's feet can be freed up should he decide to stop moving forward.

> Exercise 15: Lead with a Loose Rope
> Exercise 16: Move the Front End Over
> Exercise 17: Move the Hind End Over

Task B: *Ride your horse forward.*

> **Exercise 36: Teach a Horse to Stand Still.** Begin with the two of you sitting still. Then ask him to go forward and stay out of his way; leave him alone while he is traveling away from home.
> **Exercise 54: Ride on a Loose Rein.** Let the horse move freely forward by giving him his head.

Task C: *Cope when the horse refuses to go forward.*

> **Exercises 39 & 40: Move the Front and Hind End Over.** You will find that one end of the horse gets "stuck" more often. Free that up, then ask the horse to go forward. As soon as he does, release, and make a fuss of him.
> **Exercise 42: Focus Your Riding.** Look where you are going and take the horse there!

Note: If you get one free-flowing step away from home that is worthy of reward. During the first session, this is all you may achieve. Reward your horse, take him home. Do not think you have to go for a long ride! The fact that the horse gives you one step away from home is enough.

As long as you end the session by halting and letting him know that the free-moving step away from home is what you wanted, you have had a successful day. The next day you will get two steps. You are breaking a pattern here, so be patient. When it works you will feel a completely different attitude from the horse as you ride out of the yard.

HOW DO YOU KNOW WHEN YOU'VE DONE IT?
You and your horse will confidently leave the barn and the other horses with no hesitation.

WHAT YOU CAN DO IF IT DOESN'T HAPPEN

There is one method that seems to work very well. Place food at short intervals along a ride so that the horse travels from one "feed station" to another. Once he gets this "pattern" he will feel motivated to keep moving on, and you can start to space the feed farther apart. Don't worry if the feed is only a few feet from the yard to start with: If he freely walks out there, then you have been successful.

A. *Your horse should be happy to leave home and his pals to go for a ride with you.*

12 Jigging/Jogging on the Way Home

GOAL: To be able to turn toward home without the horse changing pace.

There is nothing more exhausting than riding a horse that knows when he's homeward bound and starts to jig/ jog and pull at the reins. It often means you both arrive hot and bothered, not a good way to end a ride.

WHY DO THIS?

To show yourself—and the horse—that *you* are in control of his feet.

HOW TO DO IT

Task A: *Be able to ride your horse forward.*

> **Exercise 42: Focus Your Riding.** Whether you're going backward or forward, you need to know where you are going and how you are going to get there.
> **Exercise 54: Ride on a Loose Rein.** Do not try to hold the horse back when he is jigging/jogging or he will just get stronger.

Task B: *Ride your horse backward.*

Every time your horse changes his pace, back him up away from home until he feels loose and soft; then ride forward. If he jigs/jogs again, repeat the exercise.

> **Exercise 38: Backing Up.** You will need to make sure the horse can back up easily before you start to try and fix this problem.
> **Exercise 60: Ride Forward and, without Stopping, Back Up.** Turn the forward jog into a backup calmly and smoothly without getting firmer in your aids. The first few times you do this the horse will resist, but once he sees that you are working to a pattern, he will forget about heading for home and start to listen to you.

The only problem I have with riding the horse backward is that he may go on for a long time before he gets quiet and soft, allowing you to ride forward again. This can cause a lot of strain on the horse's hocks, resulting in pain, which may be the only reason he stops jogging! Most horses soon get the idea that it's easier to go forward than backward, but if your horse isn't one of these, see my suggestions on p. 159.

Task C: *Remain Calm.*

Look for—and reward—even the smallest feeling you get that the horse is slowing down and listening to your request. You are not punishing him, you are simply taking control of his feet. When he jigs/jogs, he goes backward.

You need time and patience to solve this problem. You might be using *3-Minute Exercises* to set this up but the time taken to break this habit may well run into hours. But it is worth it; the key here is once you've committed to the idea, keep going!

This exercise will help you:

> **Exercise 1: Being Still Around a Horse.** Just set the exercise up and wait for the answer to come. Be very focused in what you are looking for; don't meddle with the horse while he's working this out.

HOW DO YOU KNOW WHEN YOU'VE DONE IT?

You will be able to turn your horse toward home without him changing his pace.

HELPFUL HINT

Keep a loose rein when he jogs; if you pull on him and he pulls on you it only gets worse.

WHAT YOU CAN DO IF IT DOESN'T HAPPEN

• Another technique that works well is that every time your horse changes pace, you turn him and ride in the opposite direction and as soon as he is walking calmly, you turn for home again. Repeat until the horse realizes that he, and you, are more comfortable when walking calmly and quietly.

• Slow down, be persistent. Go on shorter rides so that when you turn for home you haven't got miles to sort out. You are looking for the moment to reward him when he stops jigging/jogging even for one step. You could get off and lead him home, or let him graze or rest. Don't always ride straight in through the driveway when you arrive. Ride past it and dismount; then lead the horse back when he is calm and settled.

A. *Jigging/jogging is really a mild form of bolting and can be annoying if you don't know how to deal with it.*

13 Being Safe in Traffic

GOAL: To be able ride in traffic without fear.

Domestic horses live in the twenty-first century, so most of them need to be calm and accepting of traffic of all shapes and sizes. The place to start this training is not on the road but in a safe place where neither the horse nor the handler feels under pressure.

WHY DO THIS?

To ensure that you and your horse are always safe when riding on a busy road (fig. A).

HOW TO DO IT

Note: I advise you to use a longer rope—12 feet (4m)—when working on the ground here so if the horse gets overactive you can stay safely out of the way. But remember, the key is *not* to let him get too active in the first place!

When leading or riding on the road wear high-visibility clothing.

Task A: *Be able to lead your horse.*

> **Exercise 6: Back Up Away from You.** When a horse becomes overactive you want him to have room to move without jumping on top of you.
>
> **Exercise 12: Bend the Head Around to the Side.** Keep the horse's head flexed around *to you*; when he is looking *away* from you, he is more likely to swing his hind end toward you.
>
> **Exercise 15: Lead with a Loose Rope.** Don't have the rope so loose that the horse can move out into traffic, but know that when you hold onto a horse tightly it often makes him feel trapped, thus raising his energy level.
>
> **Exercise 20: Lead from the Off Side.** Get good at leading on both sides of your horse so that whatever side the traffic passes, *you* can be next to it. You should always be between the vehicle and the horse because, if he spooks, it will be *away* from you.
>
> **Exercise 30: Lead Through a Narrow Gap.** If a vehicle passes close to a horse he may feel trapped when there is a fence or some other type of barrier at the edge of the road. Get your horse used to passing through narrow gaps at home first.

Task B: *Cope when your horse is afraid.*

> **Exercise 1: Being Still Around a Horse.** Remain calm to give the horse confidence that you are able to look after him.
>
> **Exercise 2: Measure a Horse's Personal Space.** Be sure your horse is not scared of *anything* coming into his personal space—not just traffic. Horses and ponies that have been herded by vehicles are often more nervous about traffic coming up behind them than those who have never been moved about like this.
>
> **Exercise 3: Calculate Your Personal Space.** Are you the right person to do this training?
>
> **Exercise 4: Get a Horse's Attention.** Keep your horse's attention on you so that he can see how calm you are.
>
> **Exercise 11: Lower the Head.** This action often lowers the horse's adrenaline.

Task C: *Ride your horse in traffic, knowing that he will listen to you and remain calm.*

> **Exercise 42: Focus Your Riding.** Look where you want to go—and ride there.
>
> **Exercise 43: Ride Through a Narrow Gap.** Your horse must feel confident that he can still move forward freely even when the area he is entering appears claustrophobic.
>
> **Exercise 54: Ride on a Loose Rein.** Your instinct is to tighten your reins to prevent the horse from spooking, but often this just makes the situation worse. Maintain an even, supporting contact on the reins so that the horse does not feel under additional pressure.

HOW DO YOU KNOW WHEN YOU'VE DONE IT?

You feel safe and confident that your horse is unafraid when you are riding in traffic.

A. *The traffic you meet may be of the rather unusual kind!*

B. *Ziggy making friends with a delivery van.*

WHAT YOU CAN DO IF IT DOESN'T HAPPEN

If your horse is not comfortable being passed by cars and other vehicles, the road is not the place to train him. Get him used to traffic at home by building the learning experience something like this: Allow your horse to:

1 Inspect vehicles while they are parked (fig. B).
2 Inspect vehicles when they are parked but with the engine running.
3 Hear vehicles being started up and having their engines revved.
4 See vehicles driven away from him while he follows them.
5 I think you can begin to see how each of these are *3-Minute Exercises* building up to your horse being comfortable about walking between two parked vehicles, then two vehicles with their engines running, and so on.

6 When you start to introduce larger vehicles such as trucks and tractors try to let your horse see them first over a fence or hedge. Our horses were grazed next to a busy main road for some years and so are very safe in traffic. They have also come to love the ATV and the tractor, because they bring food!
7 Spend more time on it. Make being around vehicles a pleasant experience for you and your horse.

OTHER THINGS YOU CAN DO WITH THIS EXERCISE

Anything that worries a horse can be introduced in this way. Keep the experiences small and manageable so, if the horse is afraid, it is easy to go back to where he was calm, and start again.

14 Tying Up a Horse

GOAL: Tie your horse anywhere and know he'll still be there when you get back.

Being able to tie your horse so that you can go and do a chore is convenient and often an essential skill. If you go to shows, it means you can tie up to a trailer while you get organized.

WHY DO THIS?

Horses that don't tie are a nuisance. And, once he has learned that he can break free it becomes a very bad habit. It is possible to retrain him, but will take some time.

HOW TO DO IT

Task A: *The horse must know how to stand still.*

> **Exercise 1: Being Still Around a Horse.** Be unemotional about this: The horse needs to learn that when he is tied up he cannot get away.
> **Exercise 7: Teach Standing Still**

Task B: *The horse must give in to the pressure of the lead rope and not pull back.*

> **Exercise 15: Lead with a Loose Rope.** If your leading is solid then the next part of the training is almost done. When you tie up a horse and he doesn't pull away, it's because he is giving in to the sort of pressure that leading is all about. Should he pull back on the rope when he is tied, you want him to remember from his leading work that he must give in to the pressure, not pull.

Task C: *Attach the horse to a solid item.*

1 Take a longe line or very long rope at least 20 feet (6m) long and attach it to the halter. You will need a solid ring in the wall (or a round railing) around which the rope can easily slide.
2 Lead the horse to the ring, loop the rein through it (or around the rail), leaving about 3 feet (1m) of rope on the horse's side. Now move away, letting out the rest of the rope until you are about 10 feet (3m) from the horse, still holding onto the rope.
3 Wait. Soon the horse will attempt to move away from the ring. This will cause him to put pressure on his halter as he reaches the end of the 3-foot rope.

Do not go near the horse. You must keep hold of the end of the rope so that it does not slide or move. The horse needs to learn that he is "tied" to the ring and cannot just walk away from it. Let him feel this pressure. Most horses will test the pressure then give in to it and stand still, quite aware that they cannot break through it.

4 However, some horses really do pull so that you are unable to stop the rope from sliding through the ring. If this happens, let the rope slide but try and keep the pressure the same so that he does not feel that he has escaped from being tied up. Do not try and give a *solid* hold to his pulling but also *do not* release the rope you are holding. If you do release at this moment, you have just taught him that if he pulls on the rope he is tied with, he can escape. In other words, he has *learned* to pull back.
5 The second he stops pulling you must instantly release the rope. He will quickly realize that when he stopped going backward, the pressure stopped!
6 Go to him and lead him back to the ring and repeat the procedure. Do not reel him back to the ring: He must learn that he is always led to the place where he is to be tied up.

HELPFUL HINTS

- Keep the training area small to start with so that if the horse does run backward he will soon touch a wall or barrier with his hindquarters. This will cause him to step forward and in the process he teaches himself to give in to the pressure.
- Never *teach* a horse to tie with baler twine: A horse only has to break the twine three times to be almost impossible to tie up in the future. So please don't do it! Use my safe method to teach him, *then* you will be able to tie him to a piece of twine and rest assured he won't break it.

7 When you feel confident, start to actually tie him up properly without your holding the rope, but don't leave him unattended until you feel the moment is right.

This method of teaching a horse to tie prevents injury to the poll area behind the ears from the pressure of the halter and, in extreme cases, a horse slipping, falling, or even breaking his neck as he struggles to get away. It is actually not necessary for him to fight at all because he has already been taught to give in to pressure when being led.

Note: Never tie your horse to a solid object and let him keep pulling and fighting the rope until he realizes he cannot get away. This is a very frightening experience and, as I've already said, the horse could get seriously hurt in the process.

HOW DO YOU KNOW WHEN YOU'VE DONE IT?

You are able to tie your horse anywhere and know he'll still be there when you get back (fig. A).

WHAT YOU CAN DO IF IT DOESN'T HAPPEN

Some horses only panic and pull back when they feel the pressure around their head. Try just *draping* the lead rope through the tie ring and leaving it there. Sometimes this is enough to convince a horse that he is actually tied up.

A. *Horses should learn to be comfortable and stand quietly when tied up anywhere.*

15 Gaining and Keeping the Horse's Attention at Shows and Other Places

GOAL: The horse is relaxed when going out to different events, but still interested in the world around him.

A horse that is distracted when at an event does not make for a relaxing day. If you start introducing these experiences to the horse when he is young, he will soon get used to the hustle and bustle. But if you have a horse that hasn't had the necessary early training, you need to have some strategies for keeping his attention.

WHY DO THIS?

You need to be able to take your horse out and about, knowing that he is comfortable in new surroundings, whatever the occasion (fig. A).

HOW TO DO IT

Task A: *Gain your horse's attention from the ground as soon as you arrive.*

> **Exercise 1: Being Still Around a Horse.** The most important thing is to remain calm yourself. It is natural for a competitor to be a little excited before a class but you must try and control this heightened energy level for the sake of your horse. This takes a lot of self control and discipline. (Even as I write this I can feel my heart rate has increased. After years of competing it's a hard habit to break!)
>
> **Exercise 10: Synchronize Movement.** When you unload the horse, move slowly and deliberately as if you have all the time in the world. Accustom your horse to standing quietly in the horse trailer until you have everything ready. This takes forward planning: Make a timetable so that you know in what order you need to do things. From this you can then make a list of everything you will need for the day, and have it all packed in the right order.

But what if your horse is distracted when you unload him, looking around, perhaps calling to other horses, or running into you?

He's not doing this because he's naughty, he's doing this because he's afraid. He's in a new place with a lot of other horses and he needs to know what to do. So give him a job, which isn't letting him run around you, burning up all the energy he'll need for the competition. Put this energy to work.

When my horse becomes distracted, I start working through a series of *3-Minute Ground and Ridden Exercises* that are always the same, wherever I go. Very quickly I see him visibly relax, because it is something he understands and feels comfortable about doing.

First, I teach this routine at home, then I might try it out in the forest, on the beach, or on a visit to a friend's home, but it's always the same order. It's as though I have created a routine that puts the horse into a comfort zone where he feels secure.

So here is the list *in the order* that works for me. Feel free to adjust and adapt. If it works for you and your horse, then it's right!

> **Exercise 6: Back Up Away from You**
> **Exercise 9: Invite a Horse to Walk Toward You**
> **Exercise 15: Lead with a Loose Rope**
> **Exercise 21: Walk Forward and Backward a Specific Number of Steps**
> **Exercise 16: Move the Front End Over**
> **Exercise 17: Move the Hind End Over**
> **Exercise 18: Move a Horse Sideways**
> **Exercise 34: Change Direction While Not Moving Your Feet**
> **Exercise 35: Turn Using a Rope Over the Hocks**

By the time I've done these I'm ready to get on my horse.

Task B: *Keep your horse's attention as you ride.*
Here's the list I work through once I'm in the saddle:

> **Exercise 36: Teach a Horse to Stand Still.** If this doesn't work, I'll move right on to the other exercises and repeat this one at intervals to see if he is able to start thinking "still."
> **Exercise 37: Flex the Head Around to the Side**
> **Exercise 40: Move the Hind End Over**
> **Exercise 39: Move the Front End Over**
> **Exercise 38: Backing Up**
> **Exercise 49: Walk Forward and Backward a Specific Number of Steps**

To start with it will seem like an awful lot to do when you get to the event, but the more you practice these the quicker you'll get. You see, you are only looking for the horse to complete the *3-Minute Exercise*, not to drill him when he's done it.

So my list of nine ground exercises may take me three minutes *at the very most* because as soon as I get a loose, relaxed horse, I move on to the next exercise. The same happens with the ridden exercises, which may take even less time because I've already got the horse listening to me on the ground.

The more you practice this at home, moving on to the next exercise as soon as you've achieved looseness and softness without drilling your horse, the quicker you will get at achieving a relaxed horse that is willing to listen to you.

Task C: *Your horse needs to accept new sights and sounds.*
It will really help your horse if he has already seen many of the unusual sights and sounds in the safety of his own home: vehicles, flags, flower displays, as well as hearing loud noises and music.

Horse Agility can really help you and your horse learn to cope with the many distractions you experience at a busy event (see more about Horse Agility on p. 169).

HOW DO YOU KNOW WHEN YOU'VE DONE IT?
You can take our horse out and about, knowing that he is comfortable in new surroundings, whatever the event.

WHAT YOU CAN DO IF IT DOESN'T HAPPEN
Be honest with yourself that you've got each of the exercises solid at home—and other places less busy than at a show—before you venture out. Look at your horse management. Is he getting enough exercise to justify the amount of food you are putting into him? Does he have enough social times with other horses?

A. *Julie is helping Rupert learn that he can stand still but still look around him at a small local show.*

CONCLUSION

So, is this the end of schooling your horse for longer than three minutes?

It is the end of feeling despondent after hours of training and feeling you've achieved nothing. You always achieve *something*, so make it positive!

After reading this book, you now know you can ask the horse a question and, within three minutes, you'll get an answer. But, don't ask the question again in the same session once the horse has already answered it.

Can you imagine how annoying that must be to have the same question asked of you over and over? Instead, ask another simple question: It may be on a completely different subject or it can be related to the first one so as to build up layers of knowledge. It doesn't matter.

If you follow this working concept of variety and simple achievable tasks you and your horse will gain far more by doing less than you've ever done before!

ALSO BY VANESSA BEE

The Horse Agility Handbook: A Step-by-Step Introduction to the Sport

Horse Agility (DVD)

Vanessa Bee is the founder of the International Horse Agility Club.
You can find out more about this fast-growing sport by visiting

www.thehorseagilityclub.com

or contact the International Head Office:

Horse Agility Club HQ
The Stables
Halwill Junction
Devon EX21 5XD
United Kingdom
Phone: +44(0) 1409 221166
mail@thehorseagilityclub.com

INDEX

Page numbers in *italics* indicate illustrations.